THE 1980 GRAY MURDERS

Steve A. Reeves

TotalRecall Publications, Inc.

www.totalrecallpress.com

TotalRecall Publications, Inc..
1103 Middlecreek
Friendswood, Texas 77546
281-992-3131   281-482-5390 Fax
www.totalrecallpress.com

Cover Graphic by Roy Migabon

ISBN: 978-1-59095-580-2
UPC 6-43977-45803-2

Printed in the United States of America with simultaneously
printings in Australia, Canada, and United Kingdom.

FIRST EDITION
1   2   3   4   5   6   7   8   9   10

To Stacy, Keegan, and Kayleigh –

Thank you! Without your love and support, I would not have been able to complete this book.

To my publisher, Bruce Moran, at Total Recall Publications –

Thank you! Without your guidance and encouragement, I never would have attempted such a daunting task as writing this manuscript. I hope it's worthy of your blessing.

To my good friend, Corby Tate, at TotalRecall Publications –

Thank you! Your ability to keep everything running down the track is awe-inspiring.

To Charlotte Haynes and Renee Bennett-Morris –

Thank you! Your patience and stamina are incredible. This has been the most difficult project I've ever undertaken. I hope that I've done it justice in your eyes.

Acknowledgement

The following people were invaluable in contributing their knowledge, insights, expertise, and recollections of the events leading up to, during, and after the murders:

Lonnie Fuson, Kentucky State Police; Bo Hinkle, Jr.; Dr. George R. Nichols, II, Chief Medical Examiner, Commonwealth of Kentucky; Judy Clark, University of Louisville Medical Records Department; Earl Nicholson, Kentucky State Police; Jennifer Smith, Director of Eastern State Hospital's Personal Care Home; John Hoagland, University of Kentucky Alumni Association; Sergeant First Class Whetstone, United States Army; Rob D. Edmonds, Attorney; Pratt Hughes; Vickie L. Wise, General Counsel, Justice and Public Safety Cabinet, Office of Legal Services, Commonwealth of Kentucky; Mandy Combest, Executive's Staff Advisor, Office of the Chief Medical Examiner, Commonwealth of Kentucky; Joe Haffner, EMT-P, PHR, Director of Personnel, Rutherford County Emergency Medical Service, Miguel A. Barrera, National Personnel Records Center, National Archives and Records Administration; Shiann N. Sharpe, Official Custodian of Records, Legal Services Branch, Kentucky State Police; Lowell Lundy, Attorney; Greg Helton, Circuit Court Clerk, Knox County, Kentucky; Susan Phelps, Assistant Supervisor, Probation and Parole, Department of Corrections, Commonwealth of Kentucky; Joe Hopper, Knox Funeral Home, Barbourville, Kentucky; and Michael J. Blevins, Coroner, Knox County, Kentucky; Dennis Douda; and Justine Nguyen.

Also, I'd like to thank the many individuals who had extensive interactions with the players in this sad tragedy yet asked that their identity be kept confidential. I've honored your wish. You know who you are and I'm grateful for your assistance.

And last, but not least, I extend my deep and sincere gratitude to Charlotte Haynes and Renee Bennett-Morris. I appreciate your patience with me. You have to understand that, as I looked at the pictures of the victims, read the police files, studied the court documents, and examined the autopsy reports, it became increasingly difficult to make myself write about such a brutal occurrence in your lives. I reached the point where I began to feel like the victims were part of my family. And that made me very sad and unfocused. However, this is a story that needs to be told. I've been able to accurately determine most of the facts associated with this bloody crime. Not all, but most. To get the full story, I'd have to interview the deceased and, of course, that's not possible.

In the end, I hope you'll find, as I did, that this was a crime committed without reason. I hope that you'll feel a sense of sorrow for a mother murdered by her own son and I hope you'll shed a tear, as I did, for a young boy cut down in his prime. The assaults were vicious, bloody, and brutal. And, honestly, I'm surprised at how lightly the case was handled by the judicial system of the Commonwealth of Kentucky. At the end of the story, I'm sure you'll feel the same way.

Table of Contents

Introduction

This story is about multiple murders. Some people would say the worst kind of murders. At the time, the crimes didn't garner much media attention. Probably because they occurred in a small coal mining town without a TV or cable affiliate. However, the crime was big news to the locals because they were grisly murders and the suspect was a well-known high school football star.

Most crimes, regardless of their notoriety, seem to fade from the collective memory of a community over time. Today most people in the town of Corbin, Kentucky have not heard of the bloody atrocities that occurred in the outlying area of Gray on December 4, 1980. However, there are some town folks who will never forget and, occasionally, they will engage in tall tales, gossip, and sometimes outright lies when recounting the events of that night. Ask ten people on the street about the murders and you'll get ten different versions of a story that nobody really knows that much about. It was this pattern of inconsistencies that made me want to look further into the subject.

When I began my research, I was just naïve enough to think I could get to the bottom of the story if I went straight to the source...the person who committed the crimes. The source was a man named Riddle Cornelius Thomas, Junior. And I knew him because we had both played on the same high school football team. I sent a letter to my old teammate telling him what I was doing and asking if I could visit him in Lexington. To my surprise, a few weeks later I received a letter from him in which he agreed to speak with me. Unfortunately, before I could make travel arrangements, a family member stepped in and denied my visitation.

Although I didn't get to speak with my old teammate, I did get the assistance of several other key people – friends, family members, pastors, police officers, attorneys, EMTs, and medical doctors – who had first-hand knowledge of the criminal, the victims, the crime scene, and the aftereffects of these brutal homicides. Some of these people I will acknowledge later. Others still fear the murderer and have asked to remain anonymous.

So the question is: What actually happened on that fateful night in December, 1980? It has taken almost three years of research to put most of the pieces together and get a clearer picture. But, when all is said and done, only four people really know for sure.

Unfortunately, two of them are dead.

One is still recovering from life-threatening injuries.

And the other sits incarcerated in his room at a Kentucky facility for the criminally insane.

Prologue

Kentucky State Trooper Earl Nicholson poured the last few ounces of black liquid out of his Thermos. The warmth of the coffee radiating from the mug into his hands was a slight offset to the bitterly cold air coming through his open window. Parked next to Trooper Nicholson was a fellow officer from the Barbourville Police Department. It had been a slow night and the cops had pulled to the side of Highway 25E to catch up on the latest rumors and watch for speeders. The BPD officer was in the middle of an unflattering story on his mother-in-law when Nicholson's radio crackled to life.

"Harlan 980, dispatch."

Nicholson picked up the radio's microphone and squeezed the push-to-talk switch. "This is Harlan 980, go ahead."

"We've received a report of an automobile accident at the intersection of Highway 1441 and Portman Road in Gray. Condition of the victims is unknown. A Corbin ambulance is en route. Respond code 3."

Nicholson acknowledged the dispatcher's message. Telling his buddy that he would catch him later, the trooper downed the remaining coffee in his cup and rolled up the window. Nicholson knew the exact location of the reported wreck. Gray was a small, unincorporated, community located between Corbin and Barbourville. Of the small population who live there, most of them worked for the L & N Railroad or for one of the local strip-mining operations.

Because it was unincorporated, and had no law enforcement of its own, Kentucky State Police was usually tasked with responding to emergencies.

Nicholson looked at his watch. It was almost one o'clock in the morning; his shift was scheduled to end at 2 a.m. Turning on the emergency lights while pulling onto the highway, he thought, *"maybe this is just a minor fender-bender and I can still make it home on time."*

Trooper Nicholson stomped on the accelerator. The blaring pitch of the emergency siren drowned out the howl of the engine's turbocharger kicking in. Centerline stripes on the road zipped by as the cruiser, a white Dodge St. Regis with blue diagonal stripes on the sides, accelerated toward 100 miles per hour. Although it was an extremely dark night, the trooper was a highly trained law enforcement officer, capable of handling the risks of high-speed driving on narrow, twisting, mountain roads.

Within ten minutes of receiving the call, Trooper Nicholson was approaching the intersection of the reported wreck. He eased off the accelerator and began slowing the cruiser. In the distance, he could see the rotating beams of emergency lights flashing through leafless tree branches. As the trooper got closer, it was obvious that the source of the lights was the Corbin ambulance. Nicholson pulled in behind the emergency vehicle and parked his cruiser. Picking up the radio microphone, he reported to the dispatcher that he had arrived at the scene. Nicholson was in the process of securing the proper forms to his clipboard when he was interrupted by a knock on the window. The trooper turned to see the shivering ambulance driver, Bo Hinkle, standing on the other side of the door. Rolling down the window, Nicholson was hit in the face with a blast of air that felt like it had just come straight from the north-pole.

"Where's the crash? I don't see any cars," Nicholson said.

Hinkle replied, "We've got two fatalities but we don't have a car crash."

"What do you mean?"

The ambulance driver blew into his cupped hands before replying, "I mean we've got two dead people but they didn't die in a car crash."

It took a second before the trooper grasped the meaning of what the ambulance driver had just told him. Nicholson picked up the radio microphone and squeezed the talk button. "Dispatch, Harlan 980."

"Harlan, 980, go ahead."

"I'm now signal 7 at the Gray accident."

"Roger, 980." There was a slight pause before the trooper heard the dispatcher notify all available units to respond to his location as quickly as possible, an officer needs assistance.

Nicholson zipped up his foul-weather jacket while Hinkle opened the door. "Show me the bodies," Nicholson said, stepping out of the cruiser.

Hinkle led Nicholson through the space between the front of the trooper's cruiser and the back of the ambulance. Nicholson stopped momentarily to look through the windows on the back doors of the emergency vehicle. The medical bay was brightly lit by fluorescent light. A petite, middle-aged, woman with auburn-colored hair was lying on a gurney. She was disheveled and dirty. The dull pink pantsuit she wore was matted with brown, crispy, leaves and drying blood. A paramedic was treating her head wounds and trying to stop the flow of blood, while also attempting to calm her down. It was apparent to Nicholson that the woman was extremely agitated and on the brink of becoming hysterical.

The woman's name was Charlotte Miles Haynes.

Chapter 1

Born in Corbin, Kentucky during the first year of World War II, Charlotte Miles Haynes was welcomed into a household anchored by two college-educated parents. Her father, Howard Miles, was a short, average built man with auburn hair and hazel eyes. His friends described him as quiet, easy going, responsible, and very intelligent. To the young Charlotte, he was more of a friend than a parent.

Charlotte's mother, Jessie Laws Miles, was an independent woman and quite intelligent in her own right. She was one of the few women of her time who had gone to college and earned a Master's degree. Whereas Howard was the more hands-off parent to Charlotte and her four siblings, Jessie was the disciplinarian in the house. She took no gruff from her kids but, whenever one of them had a problem, they would seek her guidance because she always seemed to have the right answer.

By late 1942, overseas hostilities were in full swing and much of the country was changing to support the war effort. In early 1943, Charlotte's father accepted a job with the War Department and relocated his family to a small community in eastern Tennessee. Charlotte was too young to know that the town, located in a 17-mile long valley, had no official name. As she entered her toddler years, she had no comprehension of the reason her parents always made sure she was wearing the special badge issued by the government. In elementary school, Charlotte would occasionally invite a friend over to her house to play. She didn't know that her friend's parents had to fill out confidential War Department forms before her classmate arrived. In fact, it wasn't until later in her adolescent life that Charlotte was told the reason for these unusual procedures. The unnamed town was officially known to the government as the Clinton Engineer Works (after the war, the town was named Oak Ridge), and the job her father had taken involved scientific work on the Manhattan Project – the top secret undertaking of the United States to develop an atomic bomb.

Life in Oak Ridge during the war years was strict, isolated, and controlled. It was also very busy. Because the final product of the Manhattan Project was needed as quickly as possible, and because a massive amount of manpower was required to complete the task, Oak Ridge grew to be the fifth largest city in Tennessee (with the sixth largest bus transit system) within three years of breaking ground, even though the city didn't officially exist and would not show up on a U.S. map until 1949. However, the pace of population growth far exceeded the development of any municipal infrastructure. Gravel roads, wooden sidewalks, pre-fabricated houses, and the constant noise from never ending construction were the norm rather than the exception. And like the rest of the country, food, sugar, and gasoline were rationed. Understandably, there was one precious commodity in abundant supply – electricity. During the conceptualization, building, and testing of the atomic bomb, Oak Ridge was able to consume thirteen percent of the nation's electrical power thanks to the nearby Norris Dam hydroelectric plant.

To Charlotte, the town seemed like an ant colony; constant movement, people coming and going twenty-four hours a day. And from an early age, Charlotte and her siblings, along with the other children of the community, were bombarded with directives to never discuss anything they saw or heard with strangers, or for that matter, with each other. It was a world of secret codes, aliases, and lies. Secrecy demands were so essential to the success of the community that the Oak Ridge High School teams played only away games and no rosters were ever given to the opposing team.

Because Oak Ridge was basically a high-security government reservation, surrounded by barbed wire fences and patrolled by an army of armed guards (by early 1945, visible security forces included 4,900 civilian guards, 740 military policemen assigned to three detachments, and more than 400 civilian policemen[1]), parents felt safe in letting their children roam free. Charlotte took full advantage of the situation and developed into quite a tomboy. Climbing trees was one of her favorite past times. And while she was up in the branches, she thought, why not drop a twig on any unsuspecting person who ventured by?

One morning in the spring of 1952, 9-year old Charlotte was sitting in her third grade class trying to concentrate on Mrs. Porter's mathematics lesson. For the past few days it

---

[1] Charles W. Johnson and Charles O. Jackson, *City Behind A Fence, Oak Ridge, Tennessee 1942-1946* (The University of Tennessee Press, Knoxville 1981), 139

had been rainy and cold. The children had gone without recess at school and had been cooped up at home with nothing to do. But today the sun was shining brightly, it was unseasonably warm, and Charlotte's head was filled not with addition and subtraction, but with thoughts of getting outside and running barefoot through the mud. Suddenly, the principal, Mr. Evans, walked into the classroom and whispered something in the teacher's ear. The teacher had been writing equations on the blackboard and had her back to the class. But as she turned to face the students, the blood seemed to drain from her face. An air of anxiety filled the classroom. It wasn't uncommon for a student's parent to be injured doing the dangerous work down at the labs. The children sat quietly as Mrs. Porter walked back to Charlotte's desk. Kneeling down, she told Charlotte she had to go with Mr. Evans because her mother was in the office and needed her at home. Charlotte dutifully began to straighten her desk when Mrs. Porter stopped her. Go with the principal, the teacher said.

As Charlotte walked down the long hallway toward the front office, she couldn't come up with any reason why her mother would pull her out of school. Both of Charlotte's parents were highly intelligent and knew the value of a good education. In the Miles home, missing school was practically against the law. Looking up at the stern, humorless, face of the principal, she asked if she was in trouble. Mr. Evans, in a gentle, paternalistic, tone of voice replied that she wasn't. Still confused, Charlotte and Mr. Evans turned the corner that led to the principal's office. Sunlight poured through the front entryway glass and bounced off the waxed floor. Charlotte raised her hand to shield her eyes from the glare.

Once her vision had adjusted to the harsh light, Charlotte noticed her mother standing in the middle of the hall. She was wearing a dark blue pleated skirt, a white cotton blouse with tiny rose buds printed on it, and the black wedge sandals that Santa had brought her for Christmas. As Charlotte walked closer, she noticed that her mother was sobbing. The young girl was not accustomed to seeing her mother exhibit this type of sensitive emotion and the sight of tears streaming down her mother's face caused Charlotte to begin crying also. Charlotte didn't know what had happened, but she subconsciously knew it couldn't be good. Her mother dropped to her knees and cradled Charlotte's face between her hands. Brushing the hair from her daughter's eyes and wiping the tears from her cheeks, Charlotte's mother wept the words that would bring the young girl's world crashing down around her.

Chapter 2

The news of her father's death shook Charlotte to the core. The words were barely out of her mother's mouth when she felt like her heart was going to stop beating. How could her best friend be dead? He was so young, only thirty-seven years old. And just this morning hadn't he kissed her forehead and promised her that he'd be home for supper?

It took five minutes for the rest of the Miles children to be escorted from their classes to the principal's office. Charlotte stood in the school's entryway, watching the sun yield to an unexpected spring shower rolling over Black Oak Ridge. Visions of her father's smile, his laughter, filled her head. Her sorrow increased at the same rate as the rain drops that were now falling out of the sky. The principal and a few teachers grabbed umbrellas and helped Mrs. Miles load the crying children into the family's sedan. As Charlotte and her siblings – Katie, Myrtle, Maryann, and James – rode home from school, they had no way of knowing that there was a secret their father had never disclosed to the family. It wasn't a government secret that Howard had taken an oath to protect; it was a personal secret – Howard Miles was a sick man. But it wasn't a disease that could be discerned by looking at him. He grew up to be of average height and average weight, with a fair complexion and friendly brown eyes that all the girls found captivating. However, since early childhood, his heart had been slowly disintegrating.

This fact was made all too aware to him and his parents when, at age six, Howard suffered his first heart attack. Growing up, he knew that he'd never be a baseball star, or a race car driver, or an air mail pilot. He knew that his heart condition would never allow him to pursue those goals. But he did possess one incredible strength – his mind. It was an asset that he planned to use to its full potential.

Howard was an outstanding student throughout his elementary and secondary schools. He worked hard, made good grades, and eventually attended college, earning a master's degree. It was his exceptional intellect which led to Howard being offered a job by the United States War Department at the onset of World War II. The government was looking for deeply motivated, incredibly intelligent, men and women to work on a project of the highest national priority. Howard jumped at the offer and spent the war years working on the Manhattan Project – the building of the atomic bomb.

Howard knew that signing on to work for the government would be intense, but how could he reject the opportunity? Uncle Sam was picking up the expense of relocating his family to Oak Ridge, he was going to be paid an above-average salary, and his kids would have the opportunity to be educated in one of the finest school districts in the country (Oak Ridge schools were taught by teachers from 40 states and the superintendent was brought in from Columbia University. Every class in high school was taught by a teacher with a master's degree.)[2] But, most of all,

---

[2] Jay Searcy, "My Nuclear Childhood," *Philadelphia Inquirer*, August 9, 1992.

in Howard's mind it was the patriotic thing to do.

Once President Franklin D. Roosevelt was made aware of the advances being made in atomic weaponry, he declared that no expense in money, time, or manpower would be spared in the building of the bomb.[3] The pace of clearing the land, constructing the laboratories, and developing the bomb, for town that would come to be referred as Oak Ridge, was fast and furious. Up until the point where Hiroshima and Nagasaki were destroyed by atomic weapons, the professionals at Oak Ridge worked around the clock. Sometimes Howard would be at this job for exceedingly long periods of time. When he finally did come home, he was so stressed and fatigued that all he wanted was to eat and rest. Charlotte would ask her father where he'd been and what he'd been doing but, of course, he couldn't say anything to his daughter.

When the war ended in 1945, Howard was one of the few who decided that he'd stay in Oak Ridge. Several scientists formed an organization called the Federation of Atomic Scientists and petitioned Congress for civilian control of atomic power. Their legislative lobbying was instrumental in passage of the Atomic Energy Act of 1946, which created the Atomic Energy Commission and gave it jurisdiction over the control of atomic power. Union Carbide had been authorized by the AEC to manage Oak Ridge's nuclear laboratories[4] and Howard settled in to his job assisting in the development of radioisotopes that would be used for

---

[3] Jean Edward Smith, *FDR* (Random House Trade Paperbacks, New York 2007), 578-81

[4] http://www.ornl.gov/info/swords/swords.shtml

scientific research and medical treatments. However, by the early part of 1952, the stress and strain of the war years, and the added pressures of safely converting atomic energy from military use to civilian use, caught up to Howard and he died of a massive heart attack.

The day-to-day life of any widow is difficult enough. Being a young widow, and coping with the responsibility of raising three children, is a life filled with exponential hardships. There were opportunities for Jessie in Oak Ridge but after two years of getting her affairs in order, and giving the situation much thought, she decided that she'd rather be closer to family. She packed up her kids, said her good-byes to her Tennessee friends, and moved to Liberty, Kentucky.

Chapter 3

Charlotte entered 6th grade in Liberty, Kentucky. At that time, Liberty was a small farming community 80 miles northeast of Corbin, Kentucky. To her, it was culture shock to move from the hustle and bustle of Oak Ridge to the rural solitude of Casey County. Whereas Charlotte had grown accustomed to seeing the huge, multi-acre, K-25 and X-10 reactor facilities on her way to school, now the largest building she saw was the old two-story courthouse in the town square.

Charlotte did well in school. She had to – her mother, Jessie, was her teacher. When Charlotte wasn't studying or working on a school project, her mother tried to keep her busy with babysitting. Entertainment and extracurricular activities were limited in Liberty and Jessie wasn't going to have her daughter sit around with time on her hands. Jessie would entrust Charlotte with the care of her baby brother, James, and her little sister, Maryann. Charlotte would obediently comply with her mother's wishes, often enlisting some help from her younger sister, Myrtle. On the other hand, Charlotte's sister, Katie, was a constant irritant. In typical sisterly manner, the girls would spend a great deal of time bickering and trying to make life difficult for the other.

Charlotte had the quintessential 1950's childhood. Even though money was tight, her days were filled with fun, laughter, and friends. One of Charlotte's best friends was her first cousin, Henrietta. Henrietta's family enjoyed a close relationship with Charlotte's family and the two households would often get together on weekends and holidays. One of the fondest memories Charlotte has of her cousin is the time Henrietta taught her how to drive. Henrietta was two years older than Charlotte and had a 1957 Chevy. She would let Charlotte drive around Corbin and, occasionally, to Louisville when the two cousins visited relatives. Years later, Henrietta would marry a local boy. His name was Riddle C. Thomas. This union would produce a son. His name would also be Riddle C. Thomas, except everybody would come to know him as "Junior".

By the time Charlotte reached high school age, her family had left Liberty and moved to Corbin. Charlotte enrolled in Lynn Camp High School, located in the Knox county area of the tri-county town of Corbin (the other two counties located within the city limits are Whitley and Laurel). Charlotte easily made new friends and even tried out for a position on the school's cheerleader team. To no one's surprise, she made the squad on her first attempt. Over time, Charlotte's personality made her very popular with the students, especially the boys. She never had a problem finding a date for a local dance or to see the latest movie being shown at the drive-in. Among the throng of testosterone-fueled males at Lynn Camp, there was one boy in particular who always seemed to be first in line to ask Charlotte out. His name was Tommy Sisk. Charlotte had actually known Tommy since she was eleven and he was thirteen. Tommy didn't have much money so the couple would spend most of their time hanging out in group dates at church.

One day when Tommy was walking Charlotte home from church he asked her to marry him. Charlotte was only sixteen years old and a sophomore. But Tommy was eighteen, a few weeks shy of graduating from high school, and then having to report to boot camp for the Navy. He didn't want to go alone. He wanted Charlotte to come with him and the only way that could happen would be for them to get married. Charlotte sat down on the curb to think about Tommy's unexpected proposal. She wasn't in love with him but, then again, she didn't dislike Tommy. He was a good-looking boy, curly strawberry blonde hair, tall, muscular, and with the cutest freckles across the bridge of his nose. Tommy wasn't like the other boys, anxious to get out of school so they could get a job in the coal mines. No, Tommy was going places. Faraway places; places that Charlotte had only seen in pictures or read about in books. Charlotte, more out of a sense of boredom and a quest for adventure, accepted Tommy's proposal.

During the morning hours of April 4, 1959, Tommy secretly picked up Charlotte in his father's car and drove thirty-one miles to Jellico, Tennessee. Shortly after arriving in town, the couple found the local justice of the peace and eloped. That afternoon, Charlotte returned to her family as Mrs. Tommy Sisk. Her mother wasn't happy about the situation but decided not to interfere. A short time later, the happy-go-lucky life Charlotte had led as a teenage girl romping around the foothills of the Appalachian Mountains faded into her past. Charlotte found herself headed to the coastal flats of Florida as the young wife of a Navy gunner's mate.

Charlotte soon discovered that the Navy life wasn't all it was cracked up to be. During her husband's frequent deployments, she was often engulfed by a blanket of loneliness and boredom. And Charlotte hated being alone and bored. When Tommy did return, he usually had transfer orders and it was a mad scramble for Charlotte to pack up their belongings and coordinate the move to a new base. Making matters more intense was the fact that the Sisk family now consisted of seven people – Charlotte, Tommy, and their five children: Kathy, Tammie, Gene, William (called Howard by his family), and Jessie.

By the time Jessie, the youngest daughter, turned nine months old, Charlotte, who had moved the family to Ohio to be with her husband, decided she'd had enough of the Navy. And she'd had enough of Tommy, too. She and her husband divorced. Charlotte never stated the exact reason for the break-up; however, when asked if Tommy had been a good father, her response was a simple, "No."

Charlotte packed up her kids. She wasn't sure where she was going, but she knew she wanted to get away from Ohio and the negativity of being close to Tommy. Her ex-brother-in-law and his wife were moving to Florida and invited Charlotte to go with them. So, once again, Charlotte and her children found themselves living in the sunshine state.

In Florida, Charlotte found plenty of work. Initially, she got a job processing shrimp in a seafood plant. When that position didn't work out, she found employment as a school custodian in Riverview. One day, Charlotte returned from shopping to find a note pinned to the door of her double-wide trailer. The park manager wanted to speak to her. Charlotte walked down to the office where the manager informed her that she was leaving and offered Charlotte her job. Without hesitation, Charlotte accepted. This was an opportunity to make a better salary, plus she'd be closer to her kids. As a single-mother of five children, times were extremely difficult but Charlotte would do whatever it took to make the best of the situation.

It wasn't long after taking the management position at the trailer park before another man came courting. He was a tall, handsome, welder from Tampa who lived a few trailers down from Charlotte. His name was Robert Haynes. On warm, breezy, evenings she could hear him playing his guitar. And it sounded great. Charlotte's son, Howard, also played the guitar and it wasn't uncommon to see them jamming together on Robert's patio. On New Year's Eve, 1976, Robert asked Charlotte to go out with him. In later years, Charlotte would say it was the evening that she fell for the only man she's ever loved. On November 12, 1976, eleven months after their first date, Charlotte Sisk became Charlotte Haynes. Charlotte and her children, especially Howard, were the happiest they'd been in a long time.

For the next four years Charlotte focused on making the marriage work. And things seemed to be humming along quite well. So well, in fact, that Charlotte and Howard took a trip in early December, 1980, to see Jessie. Jessie had moved back to Louisville to get away from a bad second marriage and Charlotte wanted to see if there was anything she could do for her mother. She was also hoping that she'd have time to visit with Henrietta. After all, it had been almost eighteen years since she'd seen her favorite cousin. And she was certain Howard would enjoy visiting some Kentucky kinfolk.

On the morning of December 2, 1980, Charlotte, Howard, and Jessie were having breakfast in Jessie's kitchen. Shortly after 9 o'clock there was a loud knock on the front door.

Charlotte walked into the living room and cracked the door open. Fifteen year old Howard was slightly behind his mother, peering over her shoulder. Neither of them recognized the big, burly, stranger standing on the front porch. As Charlotte opened the door to ask him what he wanted, the stranger smiled and said,

"Hi. I'm Junior."

Chapter 4

Junior Thomas was a big, burly kid with speckled blue eyes and curly brown hair. He stood 5'10" and weighed 215 pounds; the perfect size for a linebacker. On any given Friday night, during the fall of 1976, that's what you'd find him doing – playing football for the Redhounds of Corbin High School. Junior led the team in several defensive categories and, as a senior, anchored a defense that helped the Redhounds win the state championship. The game of football was his only joy in life and nothing else really mattered to him. During the course of his high school career, he racked up impressive statistics; however, the prevailing opinion among the local spectators in the stands was that his success was more the result of raw aggression than any kind of football savvy.

Junior was, for the most part, well-liked by the students at CHS. He was outgoing, had a well-rounded sense of humor and, when he wanted to, he could be very persuasive. One day he asked a cheerleader if she'd like to go to a concert with him in Knoxville, Tennessee. The Marshall Tucker Band was one of his favorites and he wanted to see them perform. The girl accepted his invitation and the two of them enjoyed the hour-long drive, laughing and joking all the way to the arena. However, there was one thing Junior failed to mention to the young lady – he didn't have tickets. When they arrived at the concert site, Junior walked around the building, hand-in-hand with his date, until he found a security guard. He spent a few minutes chatting with the man. Junior finally convinced the guard to let him and his date in through a side door. Junior later stated it had been one of the best concerts he'd ever attended.

Junior may have been physically powerful and a smooth talker, but his mental capacity fell significantly short of his peers. His teachers did the best they could, even giving him additional instruction and assigning easy extra-credit projects. However, Junior struggled to obtain passing grades. He could read and write but, no matter how hard he tried, he could not pass the tests. On a stormy evening in June, 1977, Edward Elgar's *Pomp And Circumstance* played through the sound system as Junior, wearing a crimson cap and gown, walked across the stage in the high school gym. Like the rest of his classmates, he shook hands with the principal and school superintendent. However, while the other graduates were handed a folder with their gold-embossed diplomas tucked inside, Junior was handed a folder containing a blank sheet of paper. Earlier that afternoon, the yearbooks had been handed out during school. Conspicuously absent from the group photo of the class of 1977 was Riddle Cornelius Thomas, Jr.

Most people have a 5-year plan, or even a 10-year plan, after graduating from high school. That plan may include college, or attending a trade school, or acquiring work experience that will ultimately lead them down their career path. Junior wasn't thinking along those lines in the summer of 1977. His one and only goal in life was to play football for the University of Kentucky. For most people, lacking a high school diploma would force them to look at other options.

Not Junior Thomas; his thought process didn't run along the same lines as normal people. Why should he let a blank sheet of paper prevent him from being a gridiron hero in Lexington? After all, he was a very good football player, with a wall full of trophies to prove it. And why would he have to enroll in the university? He didn't want to go to any boring classes. He wanted to play ball. Surely, once he'd had the opportunity to talk to the principal, or whoever was the head of a university, and they got to know him, he wouldn't have any problem getting on the football team.

Convinced that fame and glory awaited him, Junior loaded up his black and gold Nova. Thirty minutes later, the car was speeding north on Interstate 75. Junior was on his way to tell Wildcat coach Fran Curci that his newest, biggest, meanest linebacker had arrived.

With the wooded, rolling, hills of southeast Kentucky zipping past his windows, Junior had no idea that his life was about to take an ugly and sinister turn for the worse.

Chapter 5

It was during the late summer of 1977 when Junior Thomas arrived in Lexington. He was fired up to play football for the University of Kentucky. Some people in Corbin were unaware that he hadn't actually graduated from high school and assumed that Junior had been offered a scholarship. The university denies ever having made such an offer. Junior merely showed up at the time walk-on tryouts were being held and fell in with the multitude of other aspiring players.

Seven months had passed between the time of Junior's last football game for the Redhounds and his arrival in Lexington. Seven months of eating, drinking, and avoiding any type of physical conditioning. The tryout for prospective Wildcats did not consist of the two-a-day practices that Junior had experienced in high school but, rather, grueling three-a-day sessions that were both physically and mentally challenging. Junior's lack of preparation began to show immediately. He was overweight, slow, and unable to keep up with the other players. The heat and humidity were draining. During the tackling and blocking drills, Junior was getting pounded. In all his years as an acclaimed high school player, he'd never been beaten so badly. Junior's idea of being a star football player for the University of Kentucky was not matching up with the reality of what it took to reach that goal. At the end of the first day, Junior was allowed to shower in the locker room before being called into the office of an assistant coach. The coach told him that his performance was not acceptable, cut him from the tryout squad, and wished him luck as he showed Junior the door.

Part of Junior's personality trait was his intense desire to be accepted. This is one of the reasons he enjoyed playing football so much. Under Friday night lights, dressed in his helmet and pads, Junior was praised, admired, and applauded. There is no doubt he reveled in the many awards that were presented to him.

With his dismissal from the football squad, Junior was lost and confused. He wasn't sure what he was going to do now that his football dreams had reached a dead end. He knew he didn't want to go back home. Dealing with his mother's incessant attempts to make him go to church was not an option he wanted to contemplate. If the nagging wasn't bad enough, audio tapes of fire-and-brimstone sermons were constantly being played in the house. Junior was a country boy from the hollers of southeast Kentucky, but he'd seen the bright lights of the big city of Lexington. He decided that he'd like to stick around for a while.

After his dismissal, Junior began attending late night parties with some of the football players from the university. In the beginning, his affable nature and art of persuasion allowed him access to student's dormitory rooms and fraternity houses. It's believed that during this time Junior was covertly slipped a narcotic cocktail containing PCP or "angel dust." This rumor has no basis in fact. What is known for sure is that Junior's alcohol intake increased dramatically.

Junior had always been a little "quirky", but now it became evident that his personality was turning more bizarre than ever. Nobody knew, or could understand, the reason for his mood swings. To the people who saw him wandering aimlessly around the campus, he was sullen, confused, and when "liquored up" could turn extremely aggressive without warning.

One evening, a girl, who had been friendly to Junior in high school, was sitting on the front porch of her rented house located next to the university's campus. Her roommates had gone home for the weekend. A male friend, also from Corbin, had stopped by to visit her. While enjoying their drinks, they heard a familiar voice call out from the darkness. Peering down the street, they spotted Junior walking toward them. Junior joined the couple on the porch and spent thirty minutes in an incoherent rant. At the completion of his monologue, Junior simply walked down the porch steps and melted into the night. Spooked by Junior's words and actions, the male friend refused to let the girl spend the night alone in her house. Agreeing that there was validity in her friend's concerns, especially now that Junior knew where she lived, the girl drove to her friend's apartment and spent the night on his couch.

With his friends shunning him, his football dreams evaporated, and his mental state deteriorating, Junior loaded up his black and gold Nova with his meager possessions and drove back to Corbin. What did he do when he got home? Very little by all accounts. From early 1978 through the fall of 1980, it appeared as though Junior had dropped off the social grid. A survey of friends and acquaintances confirmed that he was in town but nobody seemed to know what he was doing.

Except for the Kentucky State Police. Unable to find gainful employment legally, Junior apparently decided to make his living outside the law. As one KSP trooper stated, "We knew Junior Thomas very well; mostly from bootlegging and marijuana."

Surprisingly, there is no record of Junior being arrested for either of these offenses.

When Junior arrived in Corbin, he was hoping to get reacquainted with his ex-girlfriend. His rapidly crumbling mental state took another hit when he discovered that she was engaged. Shortly after the news was delivered to him, Junior began stalking the girl. One morning, the ex-girlfriend came out of her apartment and found a note on the windshield of her car. It was from Junior. She and Junior had split amicably and she felt that she had no reason to fear him. She smiled, put the note in her purse, and thought no more of it – until she found the next note. And the several notes that followed. According to her, "each note became more and more childish and odd. And kind of scary, too." When asked if she ever had any contact with Junior when he was stalking her, the young lady replied, "No, I never saw him. The notes just mysteriously appeared. I'd find them in the morning or sometimes when I got off work."

When word got out that Junior was stalking his former girlfriend, the young lady's friends and co-workers immediately put up a protective bubble around her. Her friends would make sure that Junior hadn't followed her to work and her co-workers would check her car in the evenings before she went home. The manager of her apartment complex was involved in her security, too. In fact, he is the only one to have actually seen Junior during this period. He was looking out his window one day when he saw Junior drive into the parking lot. Grabbing his pistol, the manager confronted Junior as he was exiting his vehicle. When he saw the pistol, he immediately returned to his car and drove away.[5]

Shortly after the incident at the apartments, the scary notes stopped. Then, in early December, 1980, the ex-girlfriend was having dinner with her fiancé when Junior walked into the restaurant. Her heart filled with dread and she held her breath as Junior approached the couple's table. To her relief, Junior was cordial to them although, according to her, "he was talking kind of whacky." After a brief conversation, he turned and walked out of the restaurant. The ex-girlfriend never saw Junior again.

She never saw him again because the next day Junior, and a couple of young men he'd befriended, went to Louisville to watch Corbin play in the state championship. Junior wasn't a high school star anymore but he still enjoyed watching football, particularly his beloved Redhounds. Besides, it was a welcome break from listening to his mother nag him about his sinful ways and his inconsistent church attendance. Before leaving, Junior's mother asked him to check on her cousin, Charlotte, while he was in Louisville. Henrietta also instructed Junior to invite Charlotte back to Corbin to visit for a while.

---

[5] According to people who knew him, Junior was extremely fearful of guns.

Chapter 6

Charlotte Haynes was anxious to see her cousin again. As Junior sped down Interstate 75, Charlotte kept glancing at her watch. In the backseat, Howard daydreamed and watched the scenery zip past his window. At first, Charlotte had been uncertain about bringing her son. He really should have been in school, but Howard was close to his mother and convinced Charlotte that it wouldn't hurt if he missed a couple of days of classes. Besides, he'd never been to Corbin and thought it would be interesting to meet some of his kinfolk.

As she sat next to him, Charlotte was amazed at Junior's transformation. The last time she'd seen him, he'd been a toddler scooting around the floor in training pants. Now, almost twenty years later, Junior had grown into a mountain of a man. At five-feet, ten-inches tall, he weighed two hundred forty-five pounds, had thick, curly, brown hair and a full beard. His body took up all of the driver's seat and spilled over onto the center armrest.

Junior and Charlotte didn't share anything in common so most of the trip was spent in small talk about family. After a three-hour drive, Junior pulled his Nova into the driveway of his mother's house on the evening of December 2, 1980. The house is located on the corner of a two-lane state road and a residential street. Two gravel driveways enter the property – one from the road, the other from the street.

Constructed in the 1960's, it's a modest, two-story house with a large front porch. Mature shade trees dot the front and back yards. Behind the house is a main line of the Louisville & Nashville Railroad. On the other side of the tracks, the terrain rises into the wooded foothills. A scattering of other houses sit on large rural lots in the surrounding area.

In the house, preparing for her guest's arrival, was Junior's mother. Henrietta[6] Thomas was forty-four-years-old and stood five-feet, five-inches tall. She had long, curly, brown hair, blue eyes, and weighed one hundred forty pounds. Not only did she and her son share the same type of hair and eye color, they also shared the same facial features. There was no doubt that she was Junior's mother. Henrietta was a deeply spiritual woman and her conservative beliefs were reflected in her manner and her clothes. She avoided flashy jewelry and fancy make-up. Some people said she dressed like a Pentecostal – even though there's no proof she belonged to that religion.[7]

Hearing the car doors slam, Henrietta rushed out of the kitchen and opened the front door. She and Charlotte rushed to embrace each other. It was a long, heartfelt hug. Momentarily pulling away from her cousin, Charlotte

---

[6] Also known as "Susan".

[7] Another person who knew Henrietta had a less flattering description of Junior's mother - "She was a little wacky and you could tell that she was 'half a bubble off' when you talked to her. She wasn't quite all there some of the time. I don't think she drank or did drugs, she just wasn't mentally all there some of the time. She would have sort of a wild/weird look in her eyes like she would look right through you sometimes – it was weird – and Junior could do the same thing."

introduced Howard to Henrietta. It was the first time Henrietta had seen the young boy. While the mothers proceeded into the house, the two sons unloaded the car. With bags in hand, Junior led Howard to the second floor and showed him the bedroom where he'd be sleeping. Then Junior went down to his first floor bedroom and unpacked.

The evening meal at the Thomas house was uneventful. Dinner was served while Charlotte and Henrietta sat at the kitchen table, talking and catching up on the latest developments in the lives of friends and family. After everybody had eaten, Howard was charged with doing the dishes – although, like all teenage boys, he complained about it. In the meantime, Junior had gone to his bedroom and shut the door. Charlotte and Howard did not see him for the rest of the night.

The next morning, Charlotte was the first to awake. She went to the kitchen to fix breakfast for everybody and was surprised to find the cupboards empty. The only food in the house was the leftovers from last night. Charlotte grabbed her purse and walked the half-mile to the corner convenience store. She purchased as much food as she could carry and walked back, arriving just as the rest of the family were waking up. Charlotte's breakfast consisted of warm cinnamon rolls and orange juice. It was one of Howard's favorite combinations.

The rest of the day was peaceful and quiet. Charlotte and Henrietta talked while Howard was outside exploring the grounds. Shortly after lunch, a coal train came rumbling down the tracks. Howard stood in the backyard and waved at the engineer. It was the biggest thrill of the day for the teenager.

Later that afternoon, Henrietta announced that she and Junior were going to church. She asked Charlotte to go with them but Charlotte declined her cousin's offer and, instead, she and Howard stayed home. While Henrietta and Junior were at church, Charlotte prepared the evening meal and called the local office of the Greyhound Bus Line. She had decided to return home the next day and she inquired about the scheduled departure times from Gray to Louisville. Around seven o'clock, Henrietta and Junior returned from church and everybody sat down to eat. Thirty minutes later, there was a knock on the door. The pastor from the church, and his wife, had come over to pray with the Thomas family. Charlotte was surprised to discover that this was a weekly occurrence. After prayers (and a little preaching), the pastor and his wife excused themselves, stating they had others of their "flock" to visit. With the eating and praying completed, Henrietta sat down at her organ and began playing gospel tunes. She asked Junior to get his guitar and join her. Soon mother and son were belting out their favorite church hymns.

Once the family concert was over, Howard and Junior went into the kitchen to play board games. Henrietta retrieved a family photo album before she and Charlotte made themselves comfortable on the couch. Sometime between nine o'clock and ten o'clock, Charlotte told Howard that it was time for him to go to bed. Howard walked upstairs to his bedroom and took off his shirt, shoes, and socks. Wearing only his corduroy pants and t-shirt[8], Howard

---

[8] According to Charlotte, Howard did not like getting fully undressed whenever he was sleeping at another person's house.

was soon asleep.

Within minutes of Howard going upstairs, Junior went to his bedroom and closed the door. Charlotte and Henrietta were sitting next to each other on the couch, deeply engrossed in the photo album. Nobody knows for sure what happened in that bedroom, but it's obvious that over the next two hours a deep, dark, murderous transformation swept over Junior.

It was half-past midnight when Junior opened his bedroom door. The two women were chuckling about a silly picture Henrietta had pointed out in the photo album. Charlotte caught a glimpse of Junior as he walked through the dining room and into the kitchen. *Must be getting a drink of water*, Charlotte thought. If she or Henrietta had been paying more attention, maybe they would have noticed the fire burning in Junior's eyes. Maybe they would have noticed the consuming anger washing over his face.

Maybe they would have noticed the 10-inch butcher knife that Junior pulled out of the kitchen drawer.

Chapter 7

"*N*o, Junior! Don't!" The word barely escaped her lips before Junior grabbed Henrietta by the hair and jerked her off the couch. Dangling from his strong grasp, toes barely touching the floor, Henrietta slapped Junior with her right hand. The blow had no effect on the stone cold hulk in front of her. Junior raised the butcher knife and plunged it into his mother, striking her in the left side, just below the armpit. Blood gushed out of the wound and splattered the photo album that had fallen to the floor.

Charlotte, momentarily stunned by the violent outburst, jumped to her feet. Grabbing Junior by the back of his jeans, she tried to pull him away from Henrietta. Junior, still holding his mother by the hair, pivoted and swung the knife at Charlotte. The first blow struck Charlotte in the head, slicing her scalp to the skull bone. The second blow caught Charlotte in the chest. Blood flowed down her face and the salmon-colored pantsuit she was wearing.

Henrietta, bleeding profusely, grabbed Junior's arm. Gasping for breath, she screamed, "Run, Charlotte! Get help!"

Charlotte let go of Junior's pants Barely able to see through the blood in her eyes, Charlotte ran through the dining room and out the back door, tripping and falling down the steps. With massive amounts of adrenaline coursing through her system, Charlotte's body didn't register the frigid, twenty-seven degree temperature. However, she did notice the house across the street with the lights on. Half-stumbling and half-running, she made her way to the front entrance. Pounding on the door, she cried out for help.

In the house, Junior's rampage continued. Now that he wasn't fighting two women, he could direct his full murderous intentions on his mother. Junior dropped his mother to the floor and sat on top of her, the weight of his body forcing the air out of her lungs. Henrietta looked into the eyes of her son and pleaded with him to not hurt her anymore. Her plea went unanswered. Without saying a word, Junior grabbed Henrietta's throat with his left hand and plunged the butcher knife into her left breast. The force was so great that the tip of the blade exited his mother's back and stuck in the hardwood floor. Henrietta cried out in excruciating pain. Junior worked the knife loose and sunk the blade into his mother again, this time striking her in the right lung. Again, the knife went all the way through her. Red, frothy, bubbles began to emerge from Henrietta's mouth and a wet, sucking, sound could be heard with each labored breath. Junior could feel the tension releasing in his mother's body. His murderous urge not yet satisfied, Junior, with both hands on the handle, buried the blade in Henrietta's right breast. Her body went completely limp. Lying in a pool of blood, the light in Henrietta's blue eyes faded to black as her heart took its last beat.

Suddenly, a voice from the other side of the room startled Junior. "What are you doing?"

Junior looked up to see Howard standing at the foot of

the stairs.

Across the street, it was becoming obvious to Charlotte that nobody was home. Bleeding and in pain, she was desperate to find help. Spotting another house on the other side of the intersection, she ran across the state road. However, before she reached the porch, a terrifying thought raced through her brain – *Howard's still in the house!*

Junior jumped off his mother's body and sprang on the small boy. Howard, sleepy and confused by the scene in front of him, didn't stand a chance. The 10-inch blade of Junior's knife tore through the young boy's right lung. Howard let out a cry and slumped to the floor, a scarlet bloom appearing on the front of his white t-shirt.

Charlotte stumbled back across the road. She'd almost reached the other side when a horrendous sight appeared – Junior was coming out the front door. Charlotte threw herself headlong into the ditch that ran between the road and the front yard. Peering through some small bushes that lined the edge of the ditch, Charlotte watched Junior carry Henrietta's dead body into the yard. Screaming like a wounded animal, Junior sat cross-legged in the grass and rocked his mother's corpse.

Charlotte's profound sadness at seeing the lifeless body of her cousin was offset by her desperation to reach her son. *How could I leave Howard?* she berated herself over and over. Now she needed to figure out a way to get past Junior. Charlotte shifted her weight in the cramped ditch. The crackle of the brittle leaves stuck to her bloody hands sounded like a gunshot in the still, cold, night. Junior instantly cocked his head. Charlotte froze, holding her breath. Junior rolled his mother's body out of his lap and walked around the side of the house. [9]

Charlotte, seeing her opportunity, crawled out of the ditch and ran to the opposite side of the house.

Charlotte entered through the back door and immediately locked it. She ran through the other rooms until she reached the front door. She made sure it was securely bolted before going upstairs to get Howard. A deep dread filled her heart when she opened the bedroom door and saw that his bed was empty. Frantically, she called his name as she clutched her bleeding chest and stumbled back down the stairs. While Charlotte was in the house, Junior was chasing down her son.

Howard had regained consciousness shortly after Junior carried his mother's body outside. Desperate to get out of the house and save himself, Howard used every bit of strength he had to leave through the back door. The freezing night air and the blood pooling in his chest cavity were slowly draining his energy. For some unknown reason, Howard headed down the driveway and toward the railroad tracks. There are scattered houses on the other side of the crossing and perhaps he was trying to make his way to one of them. Regardless of his intent, he never made it. Hearing footsteps rapidly approaching, Howard looked over his shoulder to see Junior bearing down on him. The young boy tried to run but his critically wounded body failed to respond. Howard cried, "Mom, help!", just before Junior threw the boy on the

_____

[9] The reason Junior left his mother's body is because he heard the squeak of the back screen door opening. Charlotte, her ears full of blood from her head wound, had not heard the telltale indication that somebody was exiting the house.

tracks and stabbed him in the chest. The ice cold steel of the blade sliced through Howard's left lung and pulmonary artery. The young, sixteen-year old, happy-go-lucky boy, who had told his mom that it wouldn't hurt if he missed a couple more days of classes, closed his eyes and surrendered his soul. However, Junior wasn't finished. As the last of Howard's life energy seeped out of his body, Junior stabbed him in the side of the neck. Then, in his final barbarian act, Junior slit the throat of the dead boy's body.

Chapter 8

Charlotte was half-way down the stairs when several knocks reverberated through the house. Hoping that it might be Howard trying to get back to her, she rushed to the front door and pulled aside the curtains covering the glass panes. Staring at her was the bloody figure of Junior, bellowing that he'd killed his mother and demanding that Charlotte let him in.

Disregarding her own safety, Charlotte flung open the door and yelled, "Where's my son?"

Calmly, Junior pointed to the front yard and said, "I killed him, too."

Charlotte looked in the direction Junior was pointing. In an instant, she realized her worst fear had occurred. Laying in the yard, face up, was the bloody body of Howard.[10]

In a frenzy, Charlotte rushed past Junior and ran into the yard. Straddling the young boy's legs, she raised his upper body off the cold ground and held him close to her bleeding chest. Charlotte shook her son, trying to get him to speak but Howard's head flopped backward like a rag doll. His eyes were dilated and his mouth was open, as if his final scream had been frozen in time. Gently and tearfully, Charlotte laid her son down. It was then that she noticed her cousin. Henrietta, was laying next to Howard, blood oozing out of

---

[10] While Charlotte had been in the house looking for her son, Junior had murdered Howard at the railroad crossing then carried his body back to the front yard.

her mouth and eyes.

Brutally traumatized and in shock, Charlotte stumbled back into the house. She spotted Junior standing in the bathroom, adjacent to the living room, stripped to his underwear briefs and staring at his reflection in the mirror. Not wanting to agitate him further, Charlotte decided to bluff Junior into thinking that Henrietta and Howard could still be alive.

"Junior," she said, "we've got to call somebody and get help."

Acting as if he didn't have a care in the world, Junior quietly walked over to Charlotte and wiped the blood out of her eyes. Then he turned and walked toward the front door. Still in a battered state of shock, and defying all logic, Charlotte angrily yelled at the retreating murderer, "Don't you dare leave me here by myself!"

Junior stopped, turned around, and sat on the floor. According to Charlotte, he had an expression on his face like a little boy who had been handed a million dollars. Thinking there was no better time, Charlotte picked up the telephone.

In nearby Barbourville, Earl Nicholson, a nine-year veteran of the Kentucky State Police was parked in his cruiser. Parked next to him was a local police officer. The two men were drinking coffee and discussing the evening's call-outs. It had been a slow night for both officers and Earl was looking forward to his shift ending at 2 a.m. Shortly after 1 a.m., Earl received a call from dispatch informing him there had been a multiple-injury car accident in Gray. With blue lights flashing and siren blaring, Trooper Nicholson reached Gray ten minutes after being dispatched.

However, Trooper Nicholson was not the first responder

to reach the scene. Parked in front of the Thomas house, emergency lights cutting through the darkness, was an ambulance from Corbin. Trooper Nicholson parked his cruiser behind the ambulance and gathered his accident reporting forms. Before he could open his door, the ambulance driver, Bo Hinkle, approached and motioned for Trooper Nicholson to roll down his window.

"How many do we have?" Nicholson asked, the vapor from his breath hanging in the frigid air.

"Two fatalities. One male, one female," Hinkle answered.

Not seeing any evidence of an accident, Nicholson said, "OK, where's the car?"

Hinkle glanced at the house before responding. "They didn't die in a car wreck."

It took a moment for Nicholson to grasp what the ambulance driver had said, but once he did, he picked up the police radio microphone and transmitted, "Dispatch, Harlan 980 is signal 9".[11]

Trooper Nicholson exited his cruiser. Now that he was standing, he could see in the back window of the ambulance. He noticed a bloody and hysterical female being attended to by the other medic. With flashlight in hand, Nicholson walked briefly down the driveway before cutting across the yard toward the front porch. In the cold, clear, moonless night[12], the beam from the state trooper's flashlight suddenly illuminated the bodies of Henrietta and Howard. In the

---

[11] "Harlan" indicates the trooper's assigned post. "980" was Nicholson's badge number. "Signal 9" is KSP code for officer needs immediate assistance.

[12] Hinkle later stated that it was one of the darkest nights he's ever experienced.

haunting quiet, the trooper and the ambulance driver inched up on the corpses. The deceased were lying beside each other, face up, the top half of their bodies covered in frozen blood. Howard was barefoot and bare chested[13]. Henrietta was in her cotton pajamas. Expressions of unimaginable fear and terror were frozen on the faces of the mutilated corpses. In mutual silence, Trooper Nicholson and Hinkle stared at the gruesome carnage.

The two men's thoughts and the stillness of the night air, was suddenly shattered by the slamming of the front door.

---

[13] The t-shirt he'd been wearing when he went to bed having mysteriously disappeared.

Chapter 9

The percussion from the slamming door vibrated through the bare limbs of the leafless trees. Earl and Bo's attention was immediately drawn to the source of the noise. Standing on the front porch in the sub-freezing weather was a stout, heavy-set, man. His only clothing was a pair of grungy jeans and a pair of dirty tennis shoes. Earl and Bo were unaware of the identity of the dead bodies at their feet, but they had no doubt of the identity of the man standing on the porch – Junior Thomas.[14]

Nicholson walked toward the porch at the same time Junior was coming down the steps. When Junior got within a couple of feet of him, the state trooper stopped and said, "R.C., do you know who did this?"[15]

Continuing his nonchalant stroll toward the officer, Junior said, "I did."

"Where's the knife?" Nicholson asked, as Junior was approaching the bodies.

"In the house, in the kitchen," Junior replied.

Nicholson led Junior back into the house. Upon crossing

---

[14] Nicholson had several law enforcement contacts with Junior over the previous years. Most of the incidents involved alcohol or marijuana. With gun in hand, Hinkle was the apartment manager who ran off Junior when he had been stalking his ex-girlfriend.

[15] Family and friends addressed Riddle Cornelius as "Junior". Others in the community were known to address him by his initials.

the threshold, it was evident to the state trooper that a vicious struggle had occurred in the living room. Photos from an album were strewn about and a profusion of sticky blood covered the floor. Nicholson released his grasp and told Junior to get a shirt from his bedroom. Upon returning to the living room, Junior was again asked the location of the knife. Junior said, "In there," pointing toward the kitchen.

Nicholson followed Junior into the kitchen. Up to this point, the dynamics of the interaction between the state trooper and Junior had been similar to those of a father and young son. Nicholson had issued instructions and Junior had meekly responded. However, Earl noticed a very subtle, almost imperceptible, change in Junior's expression and body language when they came to the kitchen sink. In the sink was the 10-inch butcher knife Junior had used to murder two unsuspecting people and seriously wound a third person. The knife and sink were covered in blood. Without warning, Junior picked up the knife. His eyes narrowed and a menacing expression blanketed his face.

Nicholson backed up, trying to put some distance between himself and Junior. He wanted to get outside the twenty-one foot "kill zone" of an individual armed with a cutting instrument. However, Earl's exit was blocked by a stuffed chair separating the kitchen from the living room. With his back against the chair, Earl yelled, "Put the knife down!"

Junior stared blankly at the knife. Blood from the handle oozed between his fingers.

"Put down the knife!"

Again, Junior disregarded the command.

Nicholson, sensing that the situation was now critical, placed his right hand on his holster. Unsnapping the safety latch that secured his Smith & Wesson .357 magnum, Earl again, in unmistakable language, ordered Junior to drop the knife in the sink.

It was the sound of the safety latch, and Junior's deep-seated fear of guns, that snapped him back into reality. He dropped the knife and slowly put his bloody hands behind his back.[16]

Trooper Nicholson led the handcuffed Junior out of the house. Coming down the steps, Trooper Nicholson was met by Kentucky State Police Detective Lonnie Fuson. Fuson had been the first to answer Nicholson's call for assistance. Both officers escorted Junior to Nicholson's cruiser. Once Junior was patted down to ensure he wasn't carrying any weapons, he was placed in the back seat. Just before closing the door, Fuson looked over the top of the cruiser. In the front yard he could see two white sheets covering the unmistakable shape

---

[16] A vast assortment of weightlifting equipment was found in Junior's bedroom. At the time of the murders, he had been working out for several months and was extremely strong. Trooper Nicholson stated that if his commands to drop the knife had not been followed, he was prepared to fire all six rounds of his revolver to bring down the muscular Junior.

of human bodies. Sticking his head in the cruiser, Fuson asked, "What happened, R.C.?"

Staring straight ahead, showing no signs of guilt or remorse, Junior replied in a clear, calm, voice, "I killed 'em, man."[17]

---

[17] Part of Detective Fuson's official crime scene report stated, "There was blood found in the floor in the living room next to the front door and behind the end table next to the couch. There was evidence of a struggle in the front room due to the lamp being on the couch and over turned chair. Traces of blood led out of the front door onto the front porch and out in the yard where the bodies were. There was blood found out back behind the house next to the railroad tracks."

Chapter 10

Diagram of Murder Scene

The diagram of the murder scene was drawn and submitted to the Knox County Court by Junior Thomas. It was included in a letter Junior had written to the judge proclaiming his innocence by stating that he had been "possessed" during the murders. In the diagram, he indicates that he stabbed his "aunt" in the living room. Although he did stab Charlotte in that room, she was not his aunt. He also indicates that he stabbed his mother in the front yard. This is not true. He stabbed his mother in the living room and carried her body to the front yard. Also, he's indicated that the stabbing of Howard took place at the railroad tracks. Actually, the first attack took place in the house, with the fatal stabbings taking place at the railroad tracks.

Previously, it was mentioned that Howard escaped through the back door. Technically, it was the side door, located in the refrigerator room, in which he exited the house. Charlotte was lying in the ditch in front of the bedroom at the bottom of the diagram. Due to the angle of the house, the extreme darkness, and her low vantage point, she did not see her son exit through the side door and stumble down the driveway located at the back of the house. Perhaps, if she'd been a few seconds earlier in scrambling out of the ditch, she would have seen her son before he rounded the corner of the house. Unfortunately, she'll never know if she could have saved Howard. On the other hand, there's the possibility (and she says so in her deposition) that Junior would have killed them both if he'd caught them together.

The caption of the diagram reads:

"The X's represent where the stabbings took place. The dotted line represents the route I took when I was possessed."

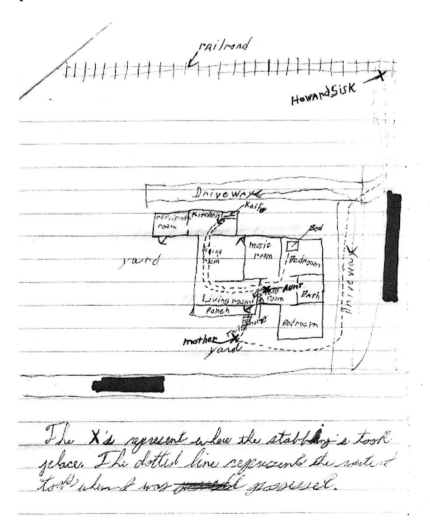

Chapter 11

Riddle C. "Junior" Thomas was booked into the Knox County Jail, Barbourville, Kentucky in the early morning hours of December 4, 1980. Later that same day, he appeared before District Judge Lewis Hopper and was arraigned on the charges of two counts of 1st degree murder and one count of 1st degree assault. Both charges were felonies and bond was set at $225,000. Nobody showed up to bail him out of jail.

During the first few hours of Junior's incarceration his demeanor was fairly mellow. However, as the day wore on, he became increasingly aggressive and unpredictable. Along with the outbursts, guards had another problem with Junior. Word had reached the jail population that the new guy was a murderer – of a woman and, more importantly, a child. Even among hardened criminals there is a "code" and that code is very specific when it comes to harming children. To be a murderer is one thing. In jail, to be the murderer of a child will get a criminal killed. The guards were in the unenviable position of preventing the murder of a murderer. The guards had also received intelligence that some of Junior's relatives, particularly on Henrietta's side of the family, were descending on Barbourville, ready to shoot Junior if he stepped out of the county lock-up.

On December 5th, Drs. George Nichols II, M.D. and Judith Cooke, M.D. completed the autopsies of Henrietta and Howard. The final diagnosis of Henrietta's autopsy stated that her body showed the following trauma: stab wound of left axilla, incisional wounds of left lung and pulmonary artery, left hemothorax, hemopericardium, stab wound of the left breast, incised wound of the right lung, right hemothorax, and stab wounds of the right breast. Indicative of Henrietta's struggle with Junior and the butcher knife he was wielding, her upper body was peppered with multiple superficial sharp instrument wounds. The cause of death was listed as "multiple stab wounds that lacerated the lung and pulmonary artery resulting in massive hemorrhage."

The final diagnosis of Howard's autopsy stated that his body showed the following trauma: multiple penetrating stab wounds, laceration of left lung and left pulmonary artery, laceration of ascending aorta, laceration of right lung apex, laceration of esophagus, bilateral hemothorax, and laceration of left common carotid and internal jugular artery. The cause of death was listed as "multiple stab wounds resulting in laceration of aorta, pulmonary artery, and lung."

The bodies of Henrietta Thomas and Howard Sisk were transported to Vankirk Funeral Home in Corbin. Henrietta's funeral was held the next day and Howard's was held on December 7th. Both ceremonies were attended by a small gathering of relatives and friends. A female member of Howard's family, overcome with sorrow and pain, collapsed during the service. After their respective funerals, Henrietta was interred in the Candle Ridge Baptist Church cemetery; Howard was buried in the Swan Pond Baptist Church cemetery. Charlotte, still undergoing treatment at the Southeastern Kentucky Baptist Hospital, was unable to attend the services for her son.

On December 9th, Junior was transported to the Laurel County jail in London, Kentucky. This modern facility was more secure than the Barbourville jail and it was better equipped to provide for inmate safety. Because of his increasingly bizarre behavior, Junior was placed under 24-hour surveillance. However, he barely had time to get accustomed to his isolation cell before Judge Hopper ordered that Junior be transported to the Grauman Forensic Psychiatry Unit in Louisville, Kentucky.

Upon admission to Grauman, Junior refused to answer questions. He remained suspicious, guarded, and uncooperative. To the psychiatrist, Dr. Ravani, he appeared to be very psychotic and delusional. From time to time, Junior exhibited behavioral problems and was placed in seclusion. Due to the apparent danger to himself and to others, he was given Thorazine on an emergency basis. During his evaluation, it was discovered that Junior had undergone psychiatric care and received anti-psychotic medication for at least a year prior to the murders.

Junior remained at the psychiatry unit until March, 1981. At that point, his evaluation time frame had expired and he was transported back to the Laurel County jail. He was diagnosed with paranoid schizophrenia and was ordered held until the court rendered a decision on the next course of action.

Chapter 12

Junior returned from Grauman with a diagnosis of paranoid schizophrenia and was deemed incompetent to stand trial. He case was moved to Knox County Circuit Court for disposition. The circuit court judge, Charles Luker, wanted his own evaluation completed and ordered Junior to be examined by two staff psychiatrists at Eastern State Hospital in Lexington, Kentucky.

On April 7, 1981, Junior arrived at the hospital on a sixty-day court order. Judge Luker requested that the psychiatrists examine him and issue an interim opinion of his competency to stand trial on the charges of murder and assault. Throughout Junior's hospital stay, he exhibited no clinically observable signs of mental disturbance. In fact, he was friendly, cooperative, and oriented. However, Junior claimed to have no knowledge or memory of the murders or assault. He told his doctors that he went to bed on the night of the crimes and the next thing he recalls is being told he was charged with murder at the police station the following morning.

At the end of Junior's hospital stay, the doctors were split on their evaluation of his mental state. One doctor stated, *"Mr. Thomas is suffering from psychosis. He is excessively preoccupied with religious ideas and admits to a past history of religious visions while awake, including hearing the voice of God. Mr. Thomas is using several defense mechanisms to avoid* emotions associated with the death of his mother. He does not experience the sense of grief and loss usually associated with the death of a loved one."

A week later, the other doctor rendered his opinion. He stated, "At present, the evaluation reveals that Mr. Thomas is not suffering from psychosis. Secondly, his alleged amnesia of the events surrounding his charges is not based on a conversion reaction. He is also using denial extensively to avoid the experience of responsibility for the death of his mother and cousin. At present, it is hard to distinguish how much he is actually remembering or not."

So the doctors were not sure if Junior was psychotic or not. However, they were in total agreement on one issue. At the end of their reports, both psychiatrists emphatically stated: "Mr. Thomas is clearly competent to stand trial."

With this bit of news, Junior was sent back to jail. This time he was remanded to the Whitley County jail in Williamsburg, Kentucky. For the next nine months, Junior's attorney tried several legal maneuvers to get his client released from custody. None of them were successful. Finally, Junior came up with an innovative way to extract himself from the dirty, noisy, dangerous confines of the county jail. Beginning in early April, 1982, he began another round of outlandish and bizarre behavior. When the guards would hand his cafeteria tray through the cell door bars, Junior would dump the food in the toilet and eat it from the steel bowl.[18] The judge promptly ordered Junior back to Eastern State Hospital.

---

[18] This behavior was reported by Detective Lonnie Fuson, Kentucky State Police.

At the hospital, Junior was, once again, stabilized. And, subsequently, deemed competent to stand trial. However, by this time, Junior had spent almost eighteen months being bounced around from jail to hospital and then back to jail. He'd had enough. On the morning of May 9, 1982, Junior Thomas simply walked out the back door of Eastern State Hospital.

The escape of a mentally ill murderer set off alarm bells throughout the commonwealth of Kentucky, especially the tri-county area surrounding Corbin.

Kentucky state troopers immediately began a manhunt for the escaped killer. Law enforcement officers in Laurel, Whitley, and Knox counties were notified to be on the lookout for Junior. Not wanting to take any chances with the safety of their constituents, the sheriffs of the tri-county area sent deputies to warn family and associates of Junior that he may be headed their way. Several people took the threat seriously enough to arm themselves with pistols and shotguns. As night fell over southeastern Kentucky, there was no sign of Junior. Tension grew in proportion to the increasing darkness.[19]

Fortunately, Junior's freedom did not last long. The next afternoon, an observant Louisville police officer spotted him nonchalantly walking down a city street. Several cops descended on the scene. Within minutes, Junior was quickly subdued and taken back into custody.

---

[19] As one family member later stated, *"I am a cousin to Junior and we lived less than a mile from him. We was terrified that he was going to come back to town when he escaped from that hospital. My grandmother was especially terrified."*

The escape set off a firestorm in the commonwealth concerning the treatment and handling of mentally ill criminals. Officials at the hospital had been warned in advance about Junior's erratic behavior, however, as Director Donald Ralph explained when interviewed by local media, "ESH is not meant to be a security facility."

Charlotte's family was extremely distressed by the escape and wanted an explanation as to how a deranged murderer could walk out of a state mental hospital. They traveled to the office of Congressman Romano Mazzoli (Kentucky's Third Congressional District, 1971 - 1995) to speak with him. Although the congressman expressed concern for the situation, he stated that there was presently nothing he could do. His follow-up letter to the family summarizes their conference:

"I certainly understand and appreciate your concern over this situation. And, I am sure there are many others who share your concerns. I would look very favorably upon the building of a facility which could adequately confine those mentally incompetent to stand trial yet who are still a threat to citizens. And, I would support federal aid to such a facility. However, the building of the facility must be a state project."

Determined to see that such a facility was built, Charlotte's family contacted the office of Governor John Y. Brown, Jr. (1979 - 1983). In August, they received his reply which stated:

"Thank you for writing me concerning the housing of accused criminals who are judged incompetent to stand trial. The Cabinet for Human Resources currently operates a facility that houses this type of individual. This facility is a maximum security psychiatric facility located within Luther Luckett Correctional Complex.

However, a non-convicted person may be kept at this Center only for the period of time necessary to complete an evaluation as to his criminal responsibility and/or his competency to stand trial. Consideration has been given to the development of a secure unit at Western State Hospital to deal with person who are considered dangerous but have not been convicted...the decision regarding such a facility, however, is contingent upon future budget appropriations."

The citizens of the Commonwealth of Kentucky were in limbo. Junior was a serious danger to the community; he just wasn't a **_convicted_** danger. However, this was about to change.

After Junior was taken into custody, he was shipped back to Eastern State Hospital; albeit under stricter security. His final evaluation, again stating that he was competent to stand trial, was forwarded to the judge. The fall session of court was scheduled to resume in October. In the meantime, Junior's legal team had worked out an agreement with the district attorney. In exchange for a guilty plea (and the district attorney not pursuing the death penalty), the charges concerning Henrietta and Howard would be amended from first-degree murder to first-degree manslaughter, and the charges concerning Charlotte would be dropped altogether.

On the morning of December 21, 1982, a little over two years for the day of the murders, Junior and his court-appointed attorney, Robert Devoe, sat in the chambers of the Knox County Circuit Court. Seated at the table to the left of them was the commonwealth's attorney, Thomas V. Handy. The bailiff call the court to order as Judge Charles Luker took his seat. The judge gave the thick file in front of him a cursory glance before asking Junior and his attorney to stand. Judge Luker asked Junior if he understood the charges against him. Junior quietly replied in the affirmative. At this point, the judge let it be known that he thought Junior to be one of the most vile, dangerous, manipulative, and disgusting person to cross the threshold of his court. With disdain in his voice, Judge Luker ordered Junior to serve a sentence of fifteen years in prison on each count of first-degree manslaughter; the sentences to run concurrently.

The Commonwealth of Kentucky now had a convicted psychotic killer...and the guards at Luther Luckett awaited their newest inmate.

Charlotte's father, Howard Miles.

Charlotte's mother, Jessie Laws Miles.

Jessie Laws Miles

Charlotte and Tommy Sisk.

Howard Sisk, 7 years old.

Howard with his sisters - Jessie, Kathy, and Beverly.

Howard Sisk, 9-years old.

Howard (right) with his brother, Gene.

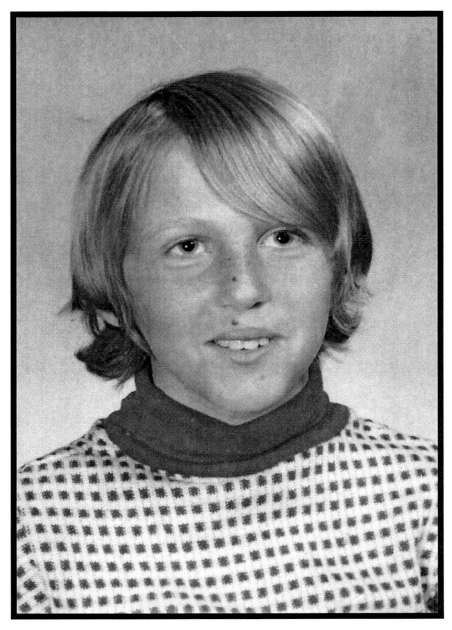

Howard Sisk, 11-years old.

Howard (right) with his brother, Gene.

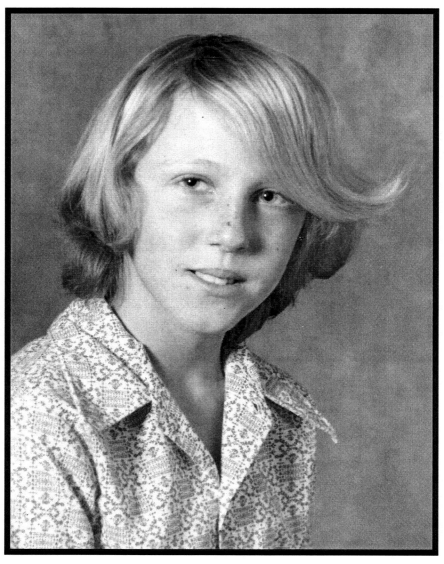

Howard Sisk, 12-years old.

Howard Sisk, 14-years old,
in his junior high school football uniform.

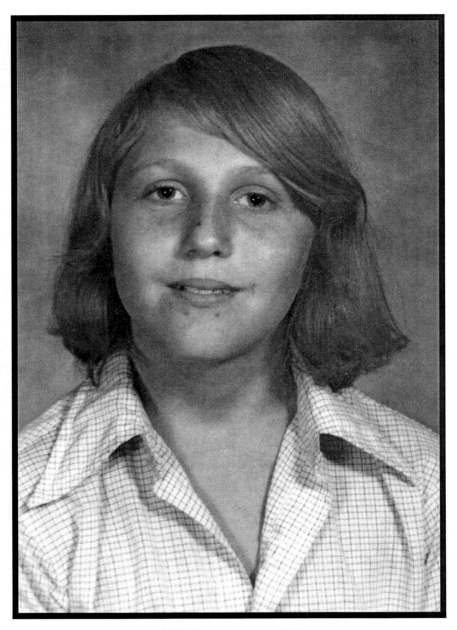

Howard Sisk, 14-years old.

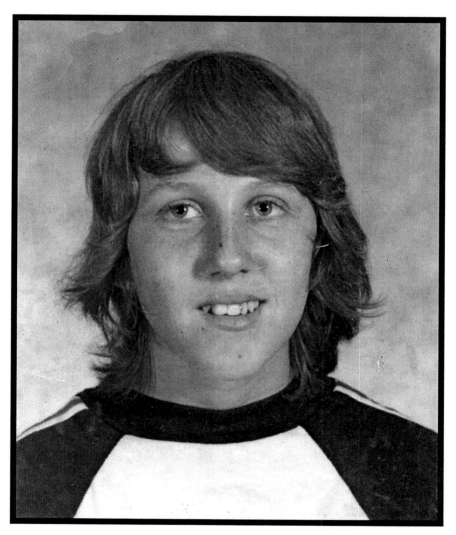

Howard Sisk, 16-years old, shortly before his murder.

Campbell Field. Home of the Corbin Redhounds.

Riddle C. Thomas Jr., 10th grade.

Junior Thomas (right foreground).
Photo by Michael Scalf.

Junior Thomas (center) receiving football award.
Photo by Debbie Young.

**Junior Thomas, final season as a Corbin Redhound.
Photo by Michael Scalf.**

Junior Thomas (center).
Photo by Debbie Young.

Charlotte, two weeks before the murders.

Kentucky State Trooper Earl Nicholson

House in which the murders occurred.

Another view of the crime scene.

**Howard Sisk escaped out the side door after
Junior's initial attack.**

Junior chased down the injured Howard Sisk
to this railroad crossing. After catching him,
Junior stabbed the young boy several more
times before cutting Howard's throat.

By the time Trooper Earl Nicholson arrived at the house,
Junior had placed the bodies of his mother and
Howard Sisk in the yard and was standing
on the front porch.

**Administration Building, Eastern State Hospital.
Lexington, Kentucky.**

Eastern State Hospital. Lexington, Kentucky.

Dormitory at Eastern State Hospital.

Howard Sisk's gravestone.

Charlotte visiting her son's grave site.

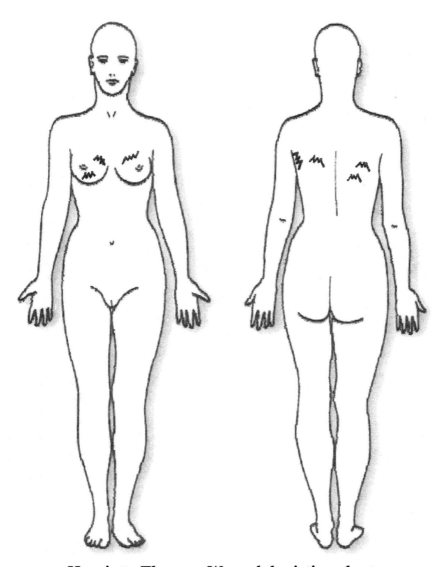

Henrietta Thomas. Wound depiction chart.

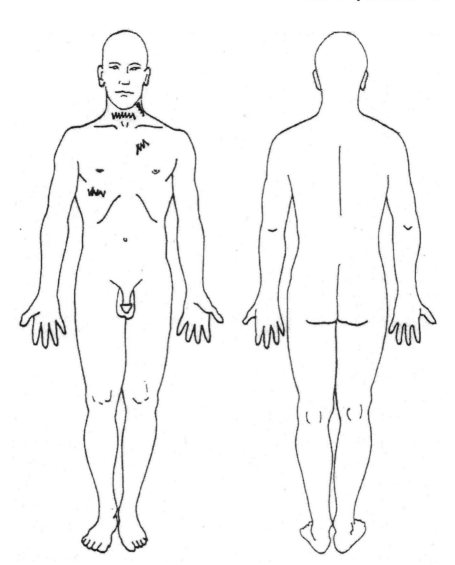

Howard Sisk. Wound depiction chart.

Epilogue

Very few people know that I had dinner with Junior a few nights before he went on that fateful trip to Louisville. I was driving down the main street in Corbin when Junior, in his old Nova, approached from the opposite direction. I waved at him and, as we passed, he motioned for me to follow him. I went around the block and caught up to him at the next traffic light. I followed him for two more blocks and, to my surprise, he pulled into the parking lot of the police station. I thought he might be in trouble and had me follow him in order to bail him out of jail. But that was not the case. We parked next to each other and exited our cars. After a few minutes of chit-chat, Junior suspiciously looked around. I instinctively looked around, too; wondering if we were under surveillance – or had the cops seen us and decided to investigate the two guys loitering in their parking lot.

Relieved that it didn't appear we were under imminent attack by the police, I turned my attention back to Junior and saw that he had opened the trunk of his car. Filling the space were bottles and bottles of whiskey, vodka, and rum. Junior was bootlegging alcohol. He asked me if I wanted to buy some and I told him I wasn't in the market that day. And besides, Junior, do you really think I'm going to buy bootlegged whiskey from you in the middle of the police parking lot?

It had been some time since I'd seen Junior so I asked him if I could buy him dinner. Without hesitation he accepted my offer. We followed each other to the old Burger Queen, which was located on what is now called the Corbin Bypass. I told Junior to order whatever he wanted. It was a quiet evening in the restaurant with just me and Junior as the only customers. We sat at a table in the middle of the restaurant and had one of the most normal conversations two people could have. Occasionally, a patron would enter the restaurant and Junior and I would tone down our language. Although Junior was broke and looking for work, he didn't seem too concerned about it. I told him that I had passed my private pilot flight test and in a few months would be heading off to the Navy to fly jets.

I'll never forget the look on his face when I told him this news. His eyes brightened and he almost sprang out of his seat with excitement. He told me that he had always wanted to fly in a plane. We talked about airplanes for a while with Junior growing giddier by the minute. He couldn't believe that he knew somebody who flew planes and he made me promise to take him flying before I left for the military. Junior's excitement got me excited, too, and I told him that I'd be happy to take him up in my airplane. We finished our meals, walked to our cars, and said our good-byes.

That was the last time I ever saw Junior.

Over the years, many of us "old" Redhounds would get together for parties, weddings, reunions, etc., and, invariably, the topic of Junior's crimes would come up. No matter how many people were in the room, it seemed there were that many variations to the re-telling of what actually occurred on the night of the murders. If there were ten people, there were ten different stories. After a while, the inconsistencies began to bother me. I wanted to know the truth. I wanted to have some sort of reason as to why my teammate would do such a horrible thing.

Three years ago, I started doing some research. I was determined to see if I could cobble together all of the opposing views and come up with an accurate portrayal of the gruesome events that occurred during the early morning hours of December 4, 1980. Requests made through the Freedom of Information Act and the Kentucky Open Records Act produced 327 pages of police reports, forensic reports, newspaper articles, correspondences, and court documents. Telephone interviews resulted in enough notes to fill two legal-sized notebooks. I even made a trip from Texas to Kentucky to visit and photograph some of the locations and institutions mentioned in this book. And I had the unintended pleasure of being physically escorted off the grounds of one Kentucky psychiatric hospital. Seems I was trespassing. However, I must say, the guard was a nice, elderly, gentleman and we had a very pleasant conversation while he was showing me to my vehicle.

As I dug into the paperwork, it didn't take long for a picture to emerge of what actually transpired in the home of Henrietta Thomas. And, believe me, it was a lot more vicious than I've been able to express in these pages. But I was still left with the question: Why?

One of the variations of the story that I've heard over the years – and it's probably the most predominant one – implies that Junior's bloody rampage was the result of a "flashback". Supposedly, somebody slipped some PCP, or Angel Dust, into his drink while he was partying at the

University of Kentucky. The story goes like this: on the night of the murders, toxins from this drug snapped something in Junior's mind and he killed two people and seriously wounded another.

As far as I can tell, there are two reasons why this story doesn't make sense. First of all, according to Richard Rudgley's, *"The Encyclopedia of Psychoactive Substances"*, the early reports of people who used PCP turning uncontrollably violent, and committing monstrous acts, was the result of ignorant media hype. Were there instances of people under the influence of PCP hurting themselves or injuring others? Yes. Were they common? No. Whatever the dangers of the drug, consistent violent behavior does not appear to be among them. Most people who have used PCP/Angel Dust express surprise that the drug is associated with violence. Additionally, there are four classifications of dose levels that affect the consciousness of the body. At low doses, the drug does not interfere with everyday task. The user is said to be "buzzed". At mid-range doses, coordination, vision, speech, pulse, and temperature are affected. The user is said to be "wasted". At high doses, a person is immobile but still conscious. The user is said to be "ozoned." And with an overdose, the user loses consciousness. Even if a person has a flashback, the degree of the flashback is based on one of the aforementioned levels of consciousness.

On the night of the murders, Junior was not "wasted" or "ozoned." He was definitely mobile (in one of his letters he stated that he was moving at 70 miles per hour) and he most certainly had the coordination needed to viciously stab three grown people and carry two of their bodies over significant distances. It's hard to believe that Junior's actions were the result of a PCP-induced flashback. And Junior was not under the influence of other drugs on the night of the murders. Shortly after his arrest, he was given a blood test. The results came back negative for illegal substances and alcohol. Neither Junior nor his attorneys ever mentioned prior PCP poisoning in official court documents.

Secondly, during my research, I discovered that Junior was mentally ill, and had been for some time. When he went to ESH after his first court appearance, it was the third time he had been admitted to the psychiatric hospital since early 1979. During the first two stays, he was stabilized (probably with anti-psychotic medications) and released to his family. Neither stabilization lasted long. And, of course, his third, and final admittance, was the result of him being charged with two counts of felony homicide and one count of felony assault.

Another interesting note concerns the use of marijuana. According to Bill Hendrick's article, *"Longtime Pot Smoking May Raise Psychosis Risk"*, in The Atlanta Journal-Constitution, "Young adults who are longtime pot smokers are more likely to have hallucinations, delusions, or to display signs of psychosis." Everyone – including the Kentucky State Police – knew Junior was a heavy pot smoker.

Most mentally ill people do not jump out of bed and kill people. So the question still remains: Why?

I contacted the Thomas family but they had no comment on the subject. On the other hand, Charlotte Haynes was willing to assist me under the following stipulation: she requested that I tell the truth, no matter what. It is with her assistance, and the help of Charlotte's granddaughter, Renee Bennett-Morris, that the following is the most accurate account of the events that led to the bloody attack of Charlotte and the gruesome murders of Henrietta Thomas and Howard Sisk:

1. On December 2, 1980, Junior Thomas drove Charlotte and Howard from their home in Louisville to visit his mother, Henrietta, in Gray, Kentucky.

2. The next day was spent with family and friends. That evening, Junior and Henrietta went to Wednesday church services. Charlotte and Howard stayed at the Thomas house.

3. After church services, the Thomas household was visited by the preacher and his wife. Junior, Henrietta, and the preacher's wife played musical instruments and sang religious songs. (Junior was a skilled guitar player.)

4. That evening, around midnight, Charlotte and Henrietta were lounging on the couch, looking at a family photo album. Junior came out of his bedroom, walked into the kitchen, and picked up a 10-inch butcher knife with a thick wooden handle.

5. Within seconds, Junior attacked Henrietta. Charlotte came to Henrietta's aid but Henrietta yelled for Charlotte to go get help.

6. With Charlotte out of the way, Junior stabbed his mother to death.

7. While Charlotte was out of the house, Howard heard the

screaming and came downstairs to investigate. Junior stabbed him and the young boy crumpled to the floor.

8. Junior picked up his mother's body and carried it to the front yard.

9. Charlotte, remembering that her son was still inside, abandoned her search for help and returned to the house. Seeing Junior coming out the front door, she hid in the ditch that ran parallel with the front yard. It was so cold – 27 degrees – that her teeth were chattering uncontrollably and the blood from her stab wounds was freezing to her skin.

10. Howard regained consciousness and ran out the back door. Junior heard the boy come out of the house and ran to the back yard.

11. Charlotte, seeing Junior run from the front yard, entered the house through the back door. She frantically searched for her son, unaware that she'd just missed seeing Howard as he struggled toward the railroad tracks.

12. Junior spotted Howard stumbling toward the railroad tracks. Junior ran the boy down and murdered him on the crossing. He then lifted the boy's body over his shoulders and carried him back to the front yard, Junior laid Howard's body next to Henrietta's.

13. Junior walked back to the front door and tried to open it. Charlotte had locked it when she first entered the house. Banging on the door, Junior yelled at Charlotte to let him in. Surprisingly, she did.

14. After opening the door, Junior told Charlotte that he'd killed her son and pointed to the body in the front yard. Charlotte cradled Howard's body, confirming that he was dead.

15. Charlotte attempted to convince Junior that Howard wasn't dead. She pleaded with him that they needed to get help. Junior allowed her to call an ambulance.

16. When the ambulance arrived, Junior greeted them from the front porch. He was wearing nothing but a pair of white underwear. Charlotte told the driver what had happened and pointed to the bodies in the front yard.

17. When the state trooper arrived, he was expecting to see an automobile accident. The ambulance driver informed him that there were two dead bodies in the front yard. The state trooper observed Junior standing on the front porch. By now, he'd put on a pair of jeans but was still shirtless.

18. Charlotte, by this time, was in the ambulance getting medical attention for her stab wounds.

19. Junior was allowed to re-enter the house to show the trooper the location of the murder weapon. Junior picked up the butcher knife. He came within seconds of being shot by the state trooper when he ignored instructions to drop it.

20. Multiple law enforcement personnel arrived on the scene. Junior calmly admitted to the killings and was taken into custody without incident.

During an interview with a friend who had known Junior and his family for several years, the subject of religion came up. This friend stated that Junior's mother, Henrietta, was extremely spiritual. She attended a church that was very evangelistic. The congregation did a lot of shouting, arm waving, and loud singing. During the week, Henrietta would play recordings of church sermons while she worked around the house. When the recordings were finished, she would tune the radio to the local gospel channel and turn the volume high enough that the hymns could be heard throughout the house. Further describing Henrietta, the friend stated, "*Henrietta was a little wacky and you could tell that she was 'half-a-bubble-off' when you talked to her. She wasn't quite all there some of the time. She would have sort of a wild/weird look in her eyes like she would look right through you sometimes – it was weird – and Junior could do the same thing.*"

When Junior returned from Lexington, his mother was constantly pleading with him to attend church services with her. And he hated it. On the evening of the murders, had Junior been dragged to church against his will? Later that night, the pastor shows up at the house. More singing and more preaching ensued. After the preacher left, Junior went to his bedroom and shut the door. What happened in that room? Had the preacher mentioned something that upset Junior? Had Henrietta, who was constantly shoving her spiritual views at her son, done something that upset him? Had Henrietta and Charlotte been overheard saying something that triggered Junior into a murderous rage? If Junior was upset with his mother, why did he kill an innocent child?

Even though the question of "why did it happen?" remains shrouded in mystery, there is no doubt of what happened.

It's been thirty-one years since the murders. Little Howard Sisk would be 45-years old; Henrietta Thomas would be 75-years old. One would be in the prime of his life, the other would be in the twilight of hers. Both of them would probably be productive members of their families and society. Unfortunately, Howard and Henrietta are dead; buried deep in the rocky southeastern Kentucky soil. Charlotte has moved to Nevada where she spends her time happily enjoying time with her grandkids. Occasionally, she'll think of that intensely brutal night in the winter of 1980 and wonder if she had stayed in the house would her son still be alive. Probably, if she had stayed in the house, Charlotte would be buried next to Howard.

Currently, Riddle Cornelius Thomas, Junior is a 52-year old resident of Eastern State Hospital. He is reported to be extremely obese and in poor health. His concurrent 15-year manslaughter sentences were completed in 1997. Why is he still housed at a mental institution?

There is no answer...only another mystery in the life of Junior Thomas.

Appendix A

Charlotte's Deposition
(Reprinted By Permission)

The deposition of Charlotte Rose Haynes was taken by agreement of the parties to this action on March 24, 1982, at the approximate hour of 12:00 o'clock noon, at the office of Lowell W. Lundy. Said deposition was taken by agreement of the parties to this action, and to be used as evidence on behalf of Plaintiffs.

The Plaintiff, Charlotte Rose Haynes, was present in person and represented by counsel, Hon. Lowell W. Lundy of Barbourville, Kentucky.

The Defendant, Riddle Cornelius Thomas, Jr., was not present in person but represented by counsel, Hon. Beecher W. Rowlette, Guardian Ad Litem, of Barbourville, Kentucky.

CHARLOTTE ROSE HAYNES appeared, and after being first duly sworn, stated and deposed as follows:

DIRECT EXAMINATION BY MR. LUNDY:

LL   Will you state your name?

CH   Charlotte Haynes.

LL   What was your maiden name, Charlotte?

CH   Miles.

LL   Where were you born?

CH   Corbin.

LL   Where do you live at the present time?

CH   About seventy-three (73) miles out of Houston.

LL   Now that's Houston, Texas, you are talking about?

CH   Yes, Texas.

LL   Charlotte, do you have children?

CH   Yes.

LL   How many do you have?

CH   I've got four (4) living.

LL   Do you have some dead?

CH   Yeah, my son's dead.

LL   What was his name?

CH   William Howard Sisk.

LL   And, how old was he at the time of his death?

CH   Fifteen (15).

LL   Now Charlotte, how did your son die?

CH   Junior stabbed him.

BR   Object. Will you state how she knows? Was she present?

LL   Well, I'm going to. She was right there. Well, go ahead. He'll object, but you go ahead.

CH   He was stabbed to death with a butcher knife by Junior.

LL   By Junior who?

CH   Thomas.

LL   Is that Riddle Cornelius Thomas, Jr., you are talking about?

CH   Yes.

LL   Were you there?

CH   I was there when he killed his mother. I had left the house trying...and he stabbed me....

LL   Well, before you get into it and tell all that...were you there present when all this happened?

CH   Yes.

LL   And, where did it happen at?

CH   In his mother's home.

LL   Is that down here at Grays in Knox County?

CH   Yes.

LL   Do you recall the date?

CH   Yeah, it was December 13th. I mean, the 3rd, I'm sorry. The 3rd. Or, early morning of the 4th.

LL   Of what year?

CH   '80.

LL   1980?

CH   Yeah.

LL   What were you doing down there?

CH   I was visiting his mother.

LL   What was his mother's name?

CH   Henrietta Susan. We'd call her Susan --- her mother's people does.

LL   Henrietta Susan Thomas?

CH   Thomas, yes.

LL   And, what kin was she to you?

CH   She's my first cousin.

LL   And, how was she your cousin?

CH   Well, her mother and my mother are sisters.

LL   And, you were visiting her?

CH   Yes.

LL   Now, who all was there at the home while you were there?

CH   You mean at the time this happened?

LL   Yeah, who all was in the house?

CH   Just me and his mother, Junior, and my son.

LL   Now, you are talking about Riddle Cornelius Thomas, Jr.?

CH   Yes.

LL   And your son?

CH   Yes.

LL   And, you and Riddle Cornelius' mother?

CH   Yes.

LL   In other words, there were only four (4) people in the house?

CH   Yes.

LL   And, what time of night did this happen?

CH   Well, the last time I looked at the clock ---- me and Susan were looking at picture albums in the living room. I was laying on the couch and she was sitting beside of me. And, I looked at the clock and it was 12:30, but this happened after that.

LL   Now, you are talking about 12:30 midnight?

CH   Yes.

LL   Was Riddle Cornelius Thomas, Jr., --- was he there, or did he come in?

CH   No, he was in his bedroom. And, my son was upstairs in his bed asleep.

LL   Were they in the same bedroom?

CH   Junior's was downstairs and my son was upstairs.

LL   Now, are you saying then that Riddle Cornelius Thomas, Jr., came out of his bedroom and did this?

CH   Yes.

LL   Had you assumed or understood or thought or seen him go to bed?

CH   I thought he went to bed, yes.

LL   And you and his mother were sitting there looking at the picture album?

CH   Yes, and talking, and I hadn't seen them in years, and we were looking at old photographs....

LL   How old was his mother, about?

CH   Forty-four (44).

LL   Now, had you seen Riddle Cornelius Thomas, that evening and before he went to bed?

CH   Yes.

LL   And, what had he been doing?

CH   Just being around.

LL   Well, did you all eat supper together?

CH   Yeah. There was a man there that had come from a church and they were talking and he stayed a while. I don't really know who he was. He was from some church out there.

LL   Well, did Riddle Cornelius Thomas, Jr. --- did he appear to be acting normal?

BR   Object.

LL   During the evening?

BR   Object. Go ahead and answer.

CH   Well, yeah. He has acted strange sometimes, but at that --- and then he acted perfectly normal. He carried on a conversation. My son even --- they played some sort of game together and he was just as normal before he went to bed as anybody else, you know.

CH   I don't really know.

LL   While you and his mother were sitting there looking at albums, I want you to just pick up and in your own words, just tell us what happened.

CH   Okay, I was laying on the couch. I pulled my shoes off, because that is where I slept. She was sitting beside me. I seen Junior going in through the dining room. See, the living room is there --- and you can see going into the dining room and to the kitchen. I thought he was getting up to get a drink of water or something. And, when he come back through I seen him in the dining room....

LL   Well, had he gone into the kitchen?

CH   Yeah, he went in the kitchen. I thought he, you know, how you would think anybody would get up to get a drink of water. And, when he come back through from the dining room he had a butcher knife in his hand, like this.

LL   Was he holding it down by his side?

CH   Yeah. Susan got up and she started trying to talk to him. And he started jabbing her in the side with the butcher knife. I jumped up from the couch and I grabbed ahold of him and tried to pull him away from her.

LL   Was he saying anything?

CH   No, he was just jabbing.

LL   Not saying a word?

CH   No. I tried to pull him...I got ahold of the back of his pants and was pulling, and he turned around sideways and started jabbing me. And, Susan got his arm back at her, and she said, "run Charlotte, get help", and I did. I went through the dining room out the back door. I tripped and fell on the stairs, you know, steps. And, I run across the road there at Grays. There is two roads. Anyway, I run across the road across this coal stuff to the house. There was one with the lights all on in it. And, I started knocking on that door and then I realized there was nobody that lived there. Then, I run next door and I beat on the door there and screamed for somebody, and then all of a sudden I remembered about Howard upstairs asleep.

LL   Is that your boy you are talking about now?

CH   Yeah. And, I turned around and I run back to the house as fast as I could. I went around by the store building that time instead of over the coal pile, and there is a road that goes by the store over here across the road. I run there, and I seen Junior out in the yard.

LL   Now, you are talking about Riddle Cornelius Thomas, Jr.?

CH   Yeah. He was carrying his mother in his arms, screaming.

LL   He was screaming now?

CH   ...saying, "Oh God" --- hollering, "Oh Lord, I've killed her", or something...I don't....

BR   Object.

LL   You go ahead and tell it. He's just objecting for the record.

CH   When I got to the highway there....

LL   Well now, let me get it straight. Where was he when you saw him then?

CH   In the front yard.

LL   And, he was holding his mother?

CH   He was carrying his mother, up in his arms, and that was just her front and top part. And, I crawled across the highway, because you know, I didn't want him to see me. There is a ditch there and the hedge grows up real high. I got down into that ditch, you know, it had leaves. I had blood on my hands, so the leaves was sticking to my hands. And, he got real quiet. I thought he heard the leaves, you know. He sat down and Susan's head was in his lap and he got real quiet and just looking around. You know how somebody will look around when they think they hear something. And, I thought well, he's heard me. And, you know, I kept thinking about those leaves, you know, I was kinda in shock, I guess, and I was worried about the leaves making a noise. And, he got up and walked real slow around the side of the house, and when he did that, I thought, well, he's going to catch me, but I've got to get back in that house. And, I run to the back door, I went in, I locked it, and I ran to the front door and locked it, and I run upstairs and my son wasn't upstairs. And, I got halfway down the stairs and he was hitting against the door. And, he said, "let me in. Let me in. You'll have to kill me now, I've killed my mother." And, I went to the front door, I opened the front door, and he said something about killing his mother and ....

LL   He was at the front door of the house trying to get in and you opened it up for him?

CH   Yes, he was beating...Yes, I opened the door for him. And, he said that --- I said, "where's Howard? Where's my son at?" And, he said, "I killed him too" and pointed to the front yard. And, I run out in the front yard and my little boy was laying out there. See, Howard had a habit when he slept at somebody's house he would pull his shoes off, but he left his own clothes on. You know, he --- that was just his way. He had everything on. He had always done that.

BR   If you'd like to take a minute and kindly...

CH   I'm just a nervous person.

LL   Go ahead.

CH   Anyway, I sat down on his legs --- my little boy's legs, and I shook him, you know, trying to get him to talk to me. And, I thought Junior had broke his neck, because you know, his little head would just go back and forth. And, I laid him back down. His eyes was open and dilated, you know. His little mouth was wide open, and I laid him back down on the ground and I looked over and Susan was laying beside of him and there was blood coming out of her mouth and eyes. I laid Howard back down, I went back into the house and Junior was standing in the bathroom --- it's right by the living room and you could see with the door open. He was standing there by the mirror in the kitchen --- I mean, in the bathroom, just standing there looking at himself, and I tried to make Junior think they were still alive, that I had to get help for them, you know. I said, "we've got to call somebody and get help." And, he come over to me and put both his hands on my a arms and took his hand and wiped blood --- you know, he stabbed me in the head and chest, and he took his hands and wiped the blood out of my face and he walked over towards the door. Now, I don't know why --- I know this don't sound normal, but when he started out that door, I hollered at him. I said, "don't you dare leave me here by myself." And, he come back and sat down on the floor with me and the way that boy looked at me --- like I had handed him a million dollars. Anyway, he sat down on the floor and I called the operator and told her, you know, that I needed help and that there had been an accident. Because, I wanted Junior to still think that they could be helped, but I wasn't...

*Author's note: break in transcript.
Page 15 of original deposition missing.

CH   Yes, on the phone. Because, you know --- well, anyway, the ambulance driver come walking and ask us for the car. And, I run to him. And, I told him --- he got me in the ambulance, and I told him what happened. So, he left me in the ambulance and he went back out, I guess, to help with the bodies. I looked back out the window of the ambulance and Junior had went inside the house and put a coat on, but he was still standing on the porch when I left.

LL   And, that was the last time you were there?

CH   They took me to the Corbin Hospital.

LL   Now, did he appear to be --- did Riddle Cornelius Thomas, Jr., after he banged on the door and you let him in there, did he appear to be normal to you then?

BR   Object.

CH   Yes.

LL   Did he talk to you coherently?

CH   Yes. He knew what had happened.

BR   Object.

CH   He told me.

LL   Do you know what ever happened to the butcher knife?

CH   I don't know. Junior didn't have it when he was at the door. I don't know. Or, at least I didn't see it. Of course, all I was wanting to see was my baby.

LL   Charlotte, where did you get cut at? Where was you stabbed?

CH   Three (3) times in the head....

LL   Now, I want you to just tell us for the record here, so that we'll know, where on your head did you get cut three (3) times?

CH   One (1) right there....

LL   Are you talking about right almost at the very top of your head?

CH   Yeah. And then one (1) here and the one (1) they had to take --- I had to go back in the hospital and have it --- they said foreign flesh and hair, and I had to have that cut out....

LL   Now, you are talking about the top back part of your head?

CH   Yeah, that one that to be cut back out. And then I had one (1) in my chest.

LL   Now, you are talking about over what?

CH   Right here.

LL   Well, that's going to be over kinda your left top of your left breast?

CH   Yeah, and one (1) on the side of the face, and in my ear.

LL   You are pointing on your left ear?

CH   Yes. It was the blood coming out of the ear.

LL   You didn't get stabbed in the ribs or anyplace?

CH   No, see, he was turned around. See, he was standing....

LL   He had his back to you and he was....

CH   Yeah, he was going like this, and I had ahold of the back of his pants.

LL   How many times did you see --- would you estimate that you saw him stab his mother?

CH   I don't know. As quick as like this. I couldn't say. How many times could you say when somebody was going like this.

LL   Well, when he came down the stairs....

CH   He was downstairs.

LL   But what I say, when he came downstairs and walked into the kitchen....

CH   No, he wasn't sleeping upstairs. He was sleeping downstairs. My baby was upstairs.

LL   Your baby was upstairs?

CH   Yeah.

LL   Well, then he had to have gone upstairs....

CH   To get Howard?

LL   ...to get your boy Howard, after...

CH   I don't know. I wasn't there. What I think is, that Howard heard me screaming and he come downstairs. I don't think that he went upstairs after him. Now, that's my idea. I don't know.

LL   But anyway, your boy Howard, --- he couldn't have been stabbed until after Susan?

CH   After Susan. Yeah. What happened to Howard happened to him from the time I was --- which couldn't have been too long --- because of the time they say, and like I told you, the last time I looked at a clock it was 12:30 and that was a little while before this happened. I don't know how long.

LL   How many times were you in the hospital?

CH   I've been in the hospital twice. At the time it happened and then I went back for....

LL   You had surgery on your head?

CH   Yeah.

LL   Do you have any...I know this is very upsetting to you and causes you a lot of emotional problems, but do you still have any kind of physical problems from it Charlotte? Does your head bother you or your ear or anything?

CH   My head hurts, but I think that I have headaches like

I've never had before, but it may be because of nerves, I don't know. I can't afford to go to the doctors, you know, for everything. But see, I've been having these headaches, you know, real bad --- migraine kindly. The kind of headaches that make you throw up, and just sick at your stomach --- and I didn't have them before, but now, I don't know whether that caused it or what, you know?

LL   Let me ask you this. How old was your boy?

CH   My boy was fifteen (15).

LL   What grade was he in?

CH   He was in the eighth (8th).

LL   How big was he?

CH   He was kinda small for his age. About like this.

LL   Okay, small for his age?

CH   Howard couldn't have done anything to Junior. Junior was two hundred fifty (250) pounds. He had weights in his bedroom.

LL   How much did your boy weigh?

CH   I really don't know. He wore size twenty nine (29) thirty (30) pants.

LL   Okay, I think that's all I want to ask her.

CROSS EXAMINATION BY MR. ROWLETTE:

BR   Did Junior have any particular expression on his face while he was stabbing his mother...

CH   I don't know.

BR   ...that you can recall?

CH   I don't --- I wasn't --- I mean, I couldn't...When he started stabbing her I automatically jumped up, and that bothers me because I automatically jumped up and grabbed her, but I didn't think of my son until I was done across that road. And, it bothers me. It bothers me a lot. But, I didn't look at his face.

BR   Did you see his face when he was stabbing you?

CH   No.

BR   You say he didn't make any statement at all while he was stabbing his mother and you?

CH   No. If he did, I didn't hear it.

BR   Did he make any statements in so far as you know, immediately prior to the stabbing?

CH The first time I heard Junior say --- well, I heard him screaming over there when he had his momma in the yard. You know, hollering "oh my God" or something of that --- you know....

BR But you don't remember exactly what he was screaming?

CH No, he was just screaming.

BR Is it safe to assume you were upset when all this was going on?

CH Of course I was upset.

BR You'd been bleeding rather proficiently, hadn't you?

CH Yes.

BR You stated that you were in shock?

CH Well, I suppose. I mean, I knew what was going on. I was perfectly aware of everything. Of course anybody that --- I mean, wouldn't you be kinda upset? Of course, I knew exactly what was going on. In fact, I'll remember that night for the rest of my life.

BR Have you ever witnessed a murder before?

CH No.

BR Have you ever been around anyone who was diagnosed as insane before?

CH   No.

BR   Do you recognize any difference in so far as the behavior of a normal person and the behavior of a so called lunatic, that you can compare them?

CH   I'm not a doctor.

BR   So, your statements then that Riddle appeared normal are more or less conjecture, it that correct?

CH   Like I said, I'm not a doctor. I don't know.

BR   Had you been around Riddle much during his lifetime?

CH   The last time I ever seen the boy was when he was a toddler. It was fifteen (15) or twenty (20) years, or something like that. He was in training pants.

BR   So then, you didn't know....

CH   I didn't know him. I wouldn't have known him had I met him on the street.

BR   Did you know what sort of behavior would be normal for Riddle?

CH   No. I had been living in Florida for years and I hadn't been around him. In fact, I seen Susan one (1) time in all those years, and he wasn't there.

BR   Susan. Now, that's Riddle's mother?

CH   Yeah. Henrietta is what everybody called her.

BR   Did you see your son outside anyplace?

CH   Just before --- or a little earlier, we were going to take a Greyhound back to Louisville the next morning, and I told Howard to go on to bed and he had gone upstairs and went to sleep sometime before that. I guess about 9:00.

BR   And, the next time you saw him he was dead?

CH   Yes, he was in the yard.

BR   Were they --- the victims, laid out side by side in the yard?

CH   Howard was laying this way, and Susan was laying this way. Her face was right up to his. See, I was sitting on his legs and when I laid him back down, she was right there.

BR   Now, is it your statement that the same Riddle Thomas who stabbed you, came over, put his hands on your shoulders and wiped the blood from your face?

CH   Yes.

BR   Did he apologize for stabbing you?

CH No. He just said, "Oh my God" and that's all. The he started to go out the door and that's when I hollered at him.

BR Did you say that he looked on his face as though you had just given him a million dollars?

CH I don't know how to explain this. You know, it's like a --- like a puppy dog, when you are petting it. You know how they'll look, and I don't know....

BR Would you say it was a look with trust?

CH Trust.

BR Did he look at you as though he trusted you?

CH ...I can't....

BR As best you can describe it. I realize you're not a ....

CH I'm not a doctor. I don't know how to explain. All I know is that he was --- at that moment I felt sorry for him.

BR You felt sorry for him?

CH Yes. Now, I don't know --- I'm not a doctor and I could not --- like you said, it was a very mixed up night.

BR   Going back to the emergency and your state of mind. Were you aware of any tension or anxiety between Riddle and his mother?

CH   No. There wasn't anything. They had been playing music.

BR   There was no tension or anxiety between yourself and Riddle or between your son and Riddle?

CH   No. None whatsoever. Everything was fine. He was playing the guitar and Susan was playing on the organ.

BR   Was he singing when he played on the guitar?

CH   No, he just played.

BR   Did he seem to be enjoying himself in so far as you could tell?

CH   Yes. Yes, everybody was....

BR   Did this preacher showing up effect his behavior in any way?

CH   No. It was early. In fact, she had the tape player running at the time when the preacher was there.

BR   Did Riddle behave as though he were a religious person, in so far as you witnessed while you were there?

CH   Yes. Like I said, that's getting into an area where....

BR   Well, I was just wondering if he talked about God or religion or anything while you were there?

CH   Yeah, Susan and --- yeah, they talked about it.

BR   Going back to your state of mind, is it safe to assume that in your normal rational thinking mind, going back to the statement you made that "I went across there and didn't even think about my son being in the house." In your normal state of mind, not excited by an emergency, your son would have been your first thought, isn't that right?

CH   Yeah. Well, I raised my children by myself and I just, you know, maybe....

BR   So, it's safe to assume then that your....

CH   As soon as I thought of him, I run back to that house. I thought, "Oh my God, Howard's upstairs." And, I turned around and I ran back to the house.

BR   Is it safe to assume then that....

CH   I knew if he heard her scream or anything, he would come down.

BR   Is it safe to assume that in your regular frame of mind you are very different from the way you were that night? You were excited, upset....

CH   I don't know. Like I said, I've never been in that kind of circumstances. I would have --- I suppose I would have tried to help her anyway, you know. It's just that Howard was upstairs, and like I said, it bothered me that I left. I mean, of course if I had had time to think, I would have run upstairs and got my son. Anybody knows that. He would have probably got us both then.

BR   Did Riddle have any reason to stab or kill your son, in so far as you know?

CH   No.

BR   Do you have any experience in the past with people who commit acts of violence against other people with no reason?

CH   No.

BR   No apparent reason?

CH   No.

BR   Based upon your lay experience, would you say that rational people go around killing people that they don't have a particular....

CH   Like I say, I'm not a doctor. I don't --- I didn't know Junior before. In my opinion, a rational person wouldn't kill somebody unless they had a reason. But, like I said, I don't know. I'm not a doctor.

BR   I understand. Have you had any counseling at all
        concerning your experience?

CH   Sometimes I think I should have. But --- I mean, I had
        nightmares for quite a while after that. But, like I
        said...that's all.

AND FURTHER THE DEPONENT SAITH NOT.

Appendix B

Junior's Letters #1

In 1980, inmates of the Kentucky State Penitentiary and the Kentucky State Reformatory filed a federal lawsuit against the Commonwealth of Kentucky. In the lawsuit, the inmates claimed that, due to overcrowding, they were being subjected to cruel and unusual punishment. They also claimed that they weren't provided with adequate vocational and educational programs to prepare them for re-entry into private life. Additionally, the lawsuit accused the commonwealth of incarcerating mentally ill patients along with the general prison population.

The commonwealth decided, rather than fight the lawsuit, they would abide by a consent decree that was negotiated with the court. Part of that decree called for the establishment of facilities capable of handling mentally ill inmates. As a result, Luther Luckett Correctional Complex, a dual-purpose institution housing the Kentucky Correctional Psychiatric Center and the Health and Family Services Cabinet was opened in March 1981. It's a 2,450-acre medium security complex located in LaGrange, Kentucky, about thirty miles northeast of Louisville. It was originally designed to house 486 inmates although, with expansions over the years, it now has an average population of 1,097.

On the afternoon of December 22, 1982, the population of KCPC increased by a factor of 1 – Riddle C. Thomas, Jr. arrived to begin serving his dual 15-year sentences that were to run concurrently. If he served his entire sentence, he'd be eligible for release in 1997.

Junior had no intention of wasting fifteen years of his life behind bars. In fact, he anticipated being home the following year to celebrate Thanksgiving with his sister. After all, he was an innocent man and an innocent man shouldn't be locked up. He should be free to do as he wishes – get a job, go to school, play football for the University of Kentucky. When Junior ended up having Thanksgiving dinner – and Christmas dinner – in the cafeteria at KCPC, he began to get antsy. With his court-appointed attorneys long gone, Junior decided to begin a letter writing campaign. Obviously, Judge Luker had forgotten he was in prison and that's the last place an innocent man should be spending his time.

A letter from Junior arrived at the Knox County Courthouse in mid-June 1984. It reads:

To Mister Judge Luker,

You may of heard some things that I might have done. But as for the things that I am charged with I didn't do. I would like for you to know that I like good things and doing what's right. I am a gentleman and I am also a human being. Human beings make mistakes. I am happy to say I am a christin. I happen to know this bible I read is true. I have read it all. When I was young I used to listen to Johnney Cash records and it would scare me to hear him sing about prison. But somehow I drifted and kindof thought a guy can break a few little laws and get away Most of the things I done against the law weren't serious but the whole point I am trying to say is this. Now that I know more about the law and penalties offenses I assure you that I will not break the law if I am aware of it. I can work and I am sure I can make just about anything. I need study about electricity and chemicals. Mechines are interesting to me. I am not mean or cruel to other people I don't see why I should waste my time in hear when I could be working and benefiting society by driving a truck or any kind of work. I have never killed anyone. I could possibly go to some college and learn more. I have had alot of girls that I like and I think when I get out I'll find one and get married. I quit smoking and I don't take drugs unless the doctor gives them to me. I want you to know that I am definitly not guilty of killing my mother and cousin even though I pleaded guilty because at that time I figured I could make parrolle nine months later. I have been locked up for 3 years 5 months & 20 some days that's a long time for something I didn't even do. I'll be honest with you I have broke some laws but nothing serious. I have been in fights using my fists sometimes in my life but really I wasn't fighting to kill anyone of those people. Let's just say I felt like I was teaching them a lesson. I am ready to be free and to not break the law if you would grant me freedom from prison. I tell you honestly that I didn't kill those people. You can check my school records, the schools I attended were Pierce School in Fort Knox Kentucky, in the first and second grade. Gray elementary school in Gray Ky. from the 3rd grade till the 8th grade and Corbin High School in Corbin Ky. Check these places and find out a lot about my past. Now somebody gets me (-?-) or says something I don't like I just try to get around without causing any trouble or having violence. Violence is wrong hurting other people I mean. But when I used to fight I wasn't aware of other people's feeling or for that matter I wasn't really aware of the laws. But now I am really aware of other people's feelings. I wasn't in many fights anyway and can't remember even hunting and searching for people to fight. Fighting people is sick thing to do but it goes on anyway but I am intelligent enough to know that it is wrong. These words express the way I feel about some things but I was really happy most of my life and it was fun. But being in prison is hard but something keeps pulling I tryed to tell you in my last letter that I am not the one responsible for those people's death. I hope you know these doctors at those hospitals were wrong when they said I was mentally ill. I'll have to say I have an imagination. But I do know what's real working for example is hard but that is a real thing and very important to a better life and life itself. I have worked hard in my life and I still have a feeling that I should be leaving the prison life as soon as you get this letter. I never physically harmed my mother anytime in my life and I still haven't. Something else other than my own mind and strength made me move that night when those people got stabbed. You and other people may not take me serious but when it all said and done your going to find that I didn't kill those people. If you want to communicate more with me notify me and we'll talk. I ask your permission to allow me to leave this prison and be free again because I didn't do the things I am charged with. I'm not mad at anybody about this but I shouldn't be blamed for something I didn't do I am really telling you the truth about this crime you have got the wrong man! Everybody makes mistakes and I've made a few that weren't really serious but being charged with killing people is and I really want you to know I didn't do this crime I am locked up for. Some foreign power other than my own caused this to happen using my body. Good-bye.

Sincerely yours
Riddle Cornelius Thomas Jr.
Send me a reply to this letter if you think you should.

Junior's Letter #2

Junior never received an answer to his June '84 letter. So in September of the same year he decided to write another and hope that he had better luck with this one.

This was the only letter where the issue of Junior facing the death penalty is mentioned.

The letter reads:

Dear Judge

I want you to know as I've told you before that I am innocent. I can be called up for another parrolle hearing if you could assist me on making parrolle I would appreciate it I have a great spirit of freedom in me. The only reason I didn't battle in court was because I thought I would get the death penalty if I failed to win my case. You know how the jury people of society can be Justice has not been done in this case. I am innocent that is the honest truth. If you can either let me go or release me on parrolle if you would please sir. Write me an answer and tell Bill Spicer to write me a letter. Thank you kindly. I am a lot better. I am in Kentucky Correction-al psychiatric hospital. I would appreciate any assisstance you could give me. I thought when I coped pleaded guilty I would surely make parrolle because I was innocent but the parrolle board seen things differently. Good bye I appreciate you time.

This letter also went unanswered.

Over the course of the next five years, Junior bombarded the court with additional letters. In these letters, a common theme emerged – Junior was an innocent man being unjustly held in prison for a crime he didn't commit. Being held against his will confused him and made him angry. In one letter to Judge Luker, he stated, *"I don't know if you understand me. I'm not the one that committed the crime. Therefore I expect to be set free and the charges dropped upon your reception of this letter."*

When Junior's claims of being innocent were ignored, he decided to switch tactics. He began writing letters proclaiming he was innocent because somebody, or something, took control of his body and made him stab three innocent people.

"I don't see how I've been locked up...because I am innocent of the charges of manslaughter. When my mother, and aunt and cousin got stabbed, something other than my own power and strength made me move. You've got the wrong man that committed the crime because somehow somebody made me move resulting in the three stabbings."

Once again, Junior's letters had zero effect on the court. Maybe a different claim would work. The next letter from Junior stated that he should be set free because he wasn't even at the scene of the murders. He had been framed.

"Judge Luker I am innocent so I don't see any reason why I should be in prison. On the night of Dec. 4th 1980 at night my Aunt and Mother and Cousin got stabbed I want you to let me out of prison. Somebody fixed it to where it would look like I was the person who did the crime. I am innocent I really am."

Finally, in May 1989, Junior must have come to the conclusion that his fate was sealed. However, he decided to write one final letter to Judge Luker. It reads:

To the Knox County Court

My name is R.C. Thomas I am writing you concerning my court case. I was charged by this court, Knox county district court and I have had to stay in prison for ten years. I am innocent of the charges. I am not the person that killed anybody, that's what I'm charged with two counts of involuntary manslaughter but I'm not the person that did it. I really am not the one that did the crime. So how can a person stay in prison for something they didn't do. I really won't out and the court can't hold me in prison for something I didn't do. If you won't to you can call a attorney for me because I won't out of prison. If you the court can't release me then I won't to appeal my case so send me information telling me what I should do concerning being released from prison. I am innocent and it should be easy to get out of prison if you are innocent

Sincerely your's
R.C. Thomas

Junior remained in prison for the duration of his sentence.

Appendix C

Junior's Father

Riddle Cornelius Thomas, Senior was born April 20, 1926. Apparently he was raised in West Virginia because, shortly after his 18th birthday, he enlisted in the United States Army, reporting for duty in Huntington. After completing boot camp in Fort Sill, Oklahoma, Senior was transferred to Camp Bowie, Texas. At Camp Bowie, he was assigned to an artillery unit stationed in Beale, California, where he was the clerk for the company commander. On June 29, 1946 the manpower requirements that had been necessary to fight World War II were no longer needed and Corporal Thomas separated from the service.

Evidently the civilian life did not suit Senior. In August, 1948, he re-enlisted in the Army and was stationed back at his old artillery unit. By 1949, Senior had risen to the rank of sergeant and was granted his request to transfer to Fort Knox, Kentucky. He spent the next 19 years as a personnel administrator and squad leader for the fort's infantry regiment.

In 1952, Senior's regiment was deployed to the Korean peninsula in response to the hostilities that had developed between North and South Korea. In April, 1953, the regiment was sent home to Fort Knox where it remained until1959. From mid-1959 through 1962, Senior was stationed in Germany (where Junior was born). In 1964, he completed a one-year tour of duty back in Korea.

Senior rose to the rank of staff sergeant, earning several medals and commendations along the way. However, in January, 1967, he became ill and was allowed to retire from the army. After processing out, Senior moved Henrietta and their children to Gray, Kentucky to be close to his wife's family.

On March 7, 1970, ten years before Junior murdered Henrietta, Senior suffered an acute heart attack and died at the Southeastern Kentucky Baptist Hospital. He is buried next to his wife in the Candle Ridge Baptist Cemetery.

About the Author

Steve A. Reeves is a native Texan who now calls Tennessee home. After graduating from Cumberland College in Williamsburg, Kentucky, he spent 28 years as a commercial pilot before retiring to spend more time with his family. He's now pursuing a second career - writing. When not sitting at his computer, Steve can usually be found with his wife and two daughters or fly fishing in one of the many east Tennessee trout streams.

CPSIA information can be obtained at www.ICGtesting.com
Printed in the USA
BVOW080029151112

305525BV00003B/209/P